THE SEPARATION

THE SEPARATION

TORN BETWEEN RASTAFARIANISM AND SOCIETAL NORMS

DESMOND TOMLINSON

MANGIFERA
BLOOM
Port St Lucie

Copyright © 2020 Desmond Tomlinson
All rights reserved.

Published by Mangifera Bloom, Port St Lucie

All rights reserved. No part of this book may be reproduced, stored, or transmitted by any means—whether auditory, graphic, mechanical, or electronic—without written permission of the publisher except in the case of brief excerpts used in critical articles and reviews.
Please send inquiries to mangiferabloom@gmail.com.

Find out more at https://www.fosteringthroughtheeyesofachild.net

1st Edition

ISBN: 978-1-7342500-0-8 (Paperback)
ISBN: 978-1-7342500-4-6 (ebook)

Library of Congress Control Number: 2020909300

Edited by Mikel Benton
Cover illustration by Michael Rohani
Book design by DesignForBooks.com

Printed in the U.S.A.

CONTENTS

THE EXORDIUM   VII

    Dedication   vii
    How My Autobiography Is Organized   x
    Conventions Used   xii
    Additional Content   xvi

ACKNOWLEDGMENT AND OVERVIEW   XVII

    Family Overview   xvii
    Child Development Agency   xviii

CHAPTER 1   HOW IT ALL BEGAN   1

    A Preview of My Father's Life and the Rastafarian Culture   2
    The Unforgettable Raid   5

CHAPTER 2   LIFE AT THE ORPHANAGE   13

    First Day Away from Home   16
    Cutting Off Our Locks   20
    The Much-Anticipated Day Finally Arrives   33

CHAPTER 3   THE ADVENTUROUS HOMECOMING   37

    Life with My Father and My Siblings   41
    Better Late than Never   53
    Back to the Old Ways of Life   57

Contents

The Unexpected 62
Cause for Concern 63

CHAPTER 4 BACK IN THE HANDS OF THE AUTHORITIES 67

Recognizing My Mother for the Very First Time 74

CHAPTER 5 HOMEWARD BOUND TO BE WITH MY MOTHER 79

Life with My Mother 82
Bye, Bye to the Good Days; Welcome to Life on the Run 86
Sleeping Outside in the Great Wide Open 88
Back under One Roof 91
The Mad Dash 93
Back under One Roof for Yet a Little While Longer 94
On the Move Once More 99
Taking Refuge inside Farm Huts 100
Relocating to Higher Grounds 104
Our Cover is Blown 110
Finally Having a Roof over Our Heads 112
Change is About to Happen 115

CHAPTER 6 RETURN TO SENDER 119

Academic Pursuits 122
The Final Departure 132

JAMAICA – THE JOURNEY 137

REFERENCES 139

THE EXORDIUM

Dedication

First and foremost, I would like to give God the glory for bestowing unto me health, strength, happiness, and the many other wonderful blessings of life. These intangible attributes have provided me with the courage and dedication to compose my autobiography. Second, I would like to take this opportunity to pay one final tribute by dedicating this volume to the memories of my only brother George Tomlinson. Other than having been addressed as Woka Man (Worker Man) by many, to everyone, he was, and will forever be, *The Unknown*. In honor of my brother's memories, I have entitled volume 2 as Woka Man. The history surrounding the Woka Man label has been documented in volume 4 of my autobiography.

I would like to commence by highlighting two of the more pressing questions that I keep pondering since the day I decided to share my life story. The first is, what defining message will my life experiences convey to humanity as a whole? And second, will humanity be receptive to such a message? I thought I had these questions all figured out, but the more I think about them, the more I realize that I may never be able to come up with definitive answers. However, in my quest to uncover the answers, I

The Exordium

would hope that you join me as I traverse the emotional, at times roller-coaster-like, journey of my life. At one point, I had thought about the possibility of conveying my story verbally. On second thought, I realized that this method would certainly not be the most effective. With that in mind, I set out to tell my story in a written form and hope to accomplish the following:

- To highlight the wonderful blessings of God that have transformed my life
- To express the overwhelming and unyielding compassion that was bestowed unto me by my foster mother, Aunt Lucy
- To establish the fact that life is not just about my inner circle or me, but also about individuals who have not been fortunate to be loved and cared for, especially throughout their early childhood and adolescent years
- To acknowledge and to credit the many individuals and institutions that have provided me with the help and support I desperately needed throughout my early childhood years
- To highlight the fact that the desire to pray and the need to persevere are the two most important characteristics that I relied on each day to overcome life's obstacles[1]

---

1 Although I have intentionally left out tangible aspects such as financial needs, it does not mean that I do not value their importance. However, the point I am conveying is this: financial and other material possessions are not characteristics of one's being. I have highlighted this concept in detail, especially throughout the compare-and-contrast sections dealing with my foster

The Exordium

- To shine a light on the foster care system and stress the need for us to develop and implement policies to protect children and the less fortunate
- The unintended consequences born by a child when there is a clash between the religious and cultural norms of society[2]
- To provide inspiration and comfort to all, particularly the less fortunate (orphans) who have gone through or find themselves going through challenging times

Although I had the burning desire to shine a light on the many aspects of my life and that of my siblings, I found myself at a crossroads, contemplating the inevitable for the following three reasons. First, I was quite fearful that I would find myself reliving the darkest and most painful memories of my past, especially those of my childhood and those concerning my only brother. Second, I wanted to live a normal life and not be misunderstood or treated any differently because of my past. Third and final, I was too busy with school, my career, my family, and the many other priorities that have taken precedence in my life. However, after many years of being nudged continuously by an internal voice, I finally decided to heed the calling and proceed with the writing of my autobiography.

Today I am more motivated than ever because I realized that someday my daughters (Julianne, Deanna, and Anna) might have the desire to learn more about the true me but I may not be around or may not have the time to

---

parents. This will become apparent in volumes 2 and 3 of my autobiography.
2 My brother and I have experienced the emotional and psychological effects as a result of these radical transformations and upheavals.

provide them with my life's story in one or two sittings. So, after thirteen long years, I have finally completed the writing of my autobiography. If my daughters have any questions concerning my childhood, I am now in a position to take the easy way out by just referring them to the four volumes that comprise my lengthy and, at times, interesting biography. Irrespective of my childhood physical and psychological struggles, I would like to see my children enjoy life to its fullest. However, I hope that they do not take life for granted, thinking that the opportunities they have today were also made available to me as a child.

How My Autobiography Is Organized

My autobiography is presented in four volumes. The first three volumes cover the unpredictable, life-changing events that occurred while I was living on the tropical island of Jamaica. The fourth reflects the transformational journey of my life after I migrated to the United States of America.

Volume 1, *The Separation* – this volume takes into account the following:

- Life with my father
- The emotional separation when my brother and I were forcefully removed from our father's care and transferred to an orphanage
- The joyous reunification when my brother and I were transferred from the orphanage back to our father's care

- The emotional separation when my brother, my sisters, and I were forcefully removed from our father's care and divvied up between orphanages
- The transfer of my brother and me from the orphanage to our mother's care
- The emotional separation when my brother and I were forcefully removed from our mother's care and returned to the orphanage

Volume 2, *Woka Man* – this volume takes into account the following:

- The transfer of my brother and me from the orphanage to a foster home
- The eternal, physical, and emotional separation that occurred when my brother was transferred to a correctional institution
- The remaining time I spent with my first foster parents, including how and why I was also removed from their care

Volume 3, *The Turning Point* – this volume takes into account the following:

- Transition to and from a temporary foster home
- When and how I was united with my wonderful, caring, loving foster mother, Aunt Lucy
- Reunion with my biological family, including my only brother

The Exordium

Volume 4, *A Dream Come True* – this volume takes into account the following:

- The continuation of my academic, professional, social, and *spiritual* journey
- The remaining precious and unforgettable time I spent with my wonderful, caring, loving foster mother, Aunt Lucy
- The journey to a land far, far away to fulfill my academic dream
- The unimaginable but inspiring and transformative academic, professional, social, and *spiritual* opportunities that continue to shape and reshape my life
- The miraculous birth of life and the family of a lifetime

Conventions Used

To maintain the originality of individual quotes, phrases, and humor, I have incorporated the Jamaican Patois (Patwa) along with the English translations. However, in some cases, I have paraphrased both the Jamaican Patois and English translations as a way to maintain contextuality. Please bear in mind that the Jamaican Patois does not have a definitive structure. Therefore, the spelling and pronunciation of certain words could differ slightly. There are many sources and variations; however, I have relied on the Jabari Authentic Jamaican Dictionary of the Jamic Language as a guide (Reynolds 2006).

As you continue to read my life story, it will become apparent that I use the word compassion quite frequently.

The Exordium

Also, it will be evident that I get a bit overjoyed when expressing my excitement as it relates to the importance of education. Although I emphasize experiences that could be perceived as insignificant, I believe that these life-changing experiences are worth mentioning because they provided me with a sense of worth, especially when compared to the more complex aspects of life. You may also uncover that my understanding of the norm differs in many ways from that of the average person. This is true because my life experiences have taught me that nothing should be taken for granted.

You will also notice that I refer to God very frequently. This is even more revealing throughout the times when things that once seemed impossible miraculously became a reality. I remember the times when I did not have a mother, father, distant family member, or even a friend to turn to for support. It was during those dark and lonely times that I discovered that praying to God was my only hope.

Although this book is my autobiography, I have taken the initiative to highlight the many acts of kindness bestowed unto me by family members, friends, acquaintances, strangers, and prominent institutions. These individuals and institutions are the many parts that have made my life whole. They have provided me with life's essentials and more. I have also been blessed to have received a lifetime of spiritual and moral support that has guided my actions and the way I perceive my fellow humankind.

Initially, I thought about composing my life story to include only the wonderful events; however, I was reminded that omitting the more painful memories would certainly not reflect an accurate picture of my life. Therefore, to

The Exordium

convey the full story and to put everything into perspective, I have decided to highlight the unfortunate situations as well.

These volumes comprise my life story in its entirety to include the past, the present, and the future. Okay, as for the future, let me be thankful for the past and the present and leave the unknown future in the hands of the Lord. I remember the day I decided to commence writing my autobiography but had no clue how or where to start. I decided that it would be a good idea to write my life story based on my recollection, then compare what I had written with the actual information recorded in my file by the Child Development Agency (CDA) of Jamaica, and the information I received from my family members and acquaintances. My rationale for this approach was simply to test the accuracy of my recollection based on my life experiences. Preceding my tenth birthday, I did not have the essential academic and social developmental skills a child of my age should have. Therefore, my recollection of this period is based mostly on random occurrences rather than a contiguous sequence of events. However, I have used the information recorded in my file to provide intelligent guesses as to the duration of such events.

After eight months of searching, in December 2009 I finally had an opportunity to review my file for the very first time. I was very impressed with the level of effort that the CDA representatives had taken to document many of events that had unfolded over the twelve years (1975 through to 1987) that I spent in the care and supervision of the Child Development Agency of Jamaica.

Before I proceed, I would like to share with you two events documented in my file that have caused me to laugh

The Exordium

out loud each time they crossed my mind. In the first, one of the CDA representatives, after visiting with me at the orphanage, recorded in my file that my teeth needed a good brushing. The CDA officer was highlighting the need for the children to maintain proper hygiene. However, in spite of the limited resources, the orphanage was not at fault because we (the children) were the ones who ate the toothpaste instead of using it to brush our teeth. In fact, whenever hunger set in, the toothpaste was one of the first edible products we would consume. I guess we were more concerned about having a clean digestive system than sporting pearly white teeth. In the second instance, the CDA representative stated that my brother and I had become homeless when the property owner deliberately took the roof off the little kitchen where we were residing with our mother. Would you believe that all this time I thought we were living out of a one-room studio! The irony of this situation is this: Why is it that my brother and I were always hungry when all this time we had been living in a kitchen?

Nonetheless, with this level of detail, I was able to fill in the missing pieces and cross-reference the information I received from my family members and friends. However, my file had a few minor omissions, such as the actual date I was transferred from the orphanage and placed in my mother's care and the day I was removed from my mother's care and returned to the orphanage. These omissions are most likely a direct result of the deterioration of my file (hard copy only).

I would hope that my life story may be an inspiration to those who find themselves in similar circumstances. I have used humor as a source of strength to block out the dreaded ordeals and painful memories that I suffered throughout my childhood years. I can assure you that these painful memories have resurfaced many times over, especially throughout the writing of my autobiography.

Irrespective of the many unfortunate circumstances, especially those concerning my only brother, I do hope that you will enjoy a smile and a little laughter as you read my tidbits of humor. I must also warn you that a number of my witticisms might go, swoosh, right over your head because they might be technologically funneled or skewed to a particular culture or era; or in the words of a teenager, they might come across as lame or botched. For the humor that you do not have a clue about, you are just going to have to wave the Google magic wand for further clarification.

Last but not least, I do believe that we can all agree that laughter is the best medicine. If you think otherwise, then please have your doctor prescribe a dose or two of this highly addictive medicine for you. And, by the way, your laughter medication is ready to be picked up at your local pharmaceutical store.

Additional Content

To complement my written autobiography, I have created the www.fosteringthroughtheeyesofachild.net website to provide additional information and content, such as pictures and links for the subjects and topics that have been portrayed throughout the different volumes. Also, the reader or interested party is more than welcome to use this website to provide an ongoing discussion regarding the content of my autobiography and other topics associated with the development and well-being of children.

ACKNOWLEDGMENT AND OVERVIEW

Please bear with me while I take this opportunity to introduce, my siblings whom I have mentioned throughout this volume of my autobiography.

Family Overview

I would like to elaborate briefly on my older siblings and me. My older siblings include Eupheme (Inez), Grace, Pauline, Paulette, and George Tomlinson. This outline of the family structure will help to put references into context. Pauline, Paulette, George, and myself will be referenced throughout this volume while Eupheme (Inez) and Grace Tomlinson will be introduced in Volume 3.

Paulette Tomlinson   Pauline Tomlinson

Throughout the early stages of our childhood, Paulette, Pauline, George, and I were subjected to our parents' Rastafarian doctrine. After many years of not being allowed to attend school, the Child Development Agency (CDA) took us from our father's care and placed

Acknowledgment and Overview

My brother and I, from right to left, respectively.
Picture date: 1979

us in different orphanages. My sisters were placed in one orphanage, while my brother and I were placed in another. After experiencing a roller-coaster-like, back-and-forth transition among our father, the orphanage, and our mother's care, the CDA finally transferred my brother and me to a foster home. The details of our foster care experience are documented in volume 2.

Pauline and Paulette Tomlinson are my twin sisters. As of today, Paulette has three daughters, and Pauline has two sons. They spent many years of their adolescent life being shuttled in and out of orphanages. Today they both are struggling to cope because they did not have the opportunity to acquire the desired level of education. This limitation has severely affected their ability to gain any meaningful employment. Despite the many hurdles and daily challenges they have had to overcome, they always display warm and pleasant smiles.

Child Development Agency

I would like to extend my sincere thanks and deepest gratitude to the members of the Child Development Agency (CDA) of Jamaica. They went above and beyond their call of duty to make my well-being their priority. This dedicated group of individuals worked tirelessly on my behalf from the very day (August 13, 1975) I was assigned to their care through to the day (August 13, 1987) I received my honorable discharge from the foster care system.

Finally, I would like to extend my sincere thanks and gratitude to all my fellow Jamaicans and the many charitable organizations for helping me to realize my dreams. Without your tax participation and other forms of charitable contributions (especially throughout the time I spent at the orphanage), it would not have been possible for me to acquire life's essentials and more. Your moral and financial support is what kept me going. Besides, I am grateful that you have supported my academic dreams both in Jamaica and in the United States of America. So next time you notice that your paystub reflects a little less take-home amount, it is because of someone like me who was totally dependent on someone like you. Orphan children gotta eat too. I would like to remind you that when I was hungry, you gave me food; when I was thirsty, you gave me a drink; and when I was homeless, you provided a home for me. Therefore, I can say with much sincerity that your kindness and outstanding support have not been and will not be forgotten.

CHAPTER 1

HOW IT ALL BEGAN

Now that I have given you a glimpse into the future, I will take you back to where it all began. The recollection of my life's journey commenced while I was living with my father, Clement Tomlinson, and my three older siblings, Pauline, Paulette, and George Tomlinson, in Darliston, Westmoreland, Jamaica. My twin sisters, Pauline and Paulette, were fourteen years old, followed by my brother and me, who were nine and seven years old, respectively. Throughout this phase of my early childhood, I had no recollection of ever seeing a mother, nor was I aware that my family structure was missing the most important member.

Our father subjected us to a strict version of the Rastafarian doctrine. In Jamaica, Rastafarians are also known as Rasta or Dreadlocks. Dreadlocks, or Locks, is a term used to describe Rastafarians with uncombed, nappy hair. We were brought up in this manner because our father embraced the Rastafarian doctrine passionately. In fact, the Rastafarian doctrine was woven into our every way of life.

Chapter 1

A Preview of My Father's Life and the Rastafarian Culture

Seeing that my father had such a profound impact on my life throughout my early childhood, I would like to take some time to focus on his life as a parent and his philosophies, as they pertain to the Rastafarian culture and doctrine.

The Rastafarian doctrine is based on the teachings of Marcus Garvey (1920s, Jamaica) and coronation of Haile Selassie (1930, Ethiopia)[3] (ReligionFacts). Although there are other forms of Rastafarian practices and beliefs, the ReligionFacts website overview (as outlined in the footnote) of the Rastafarian culture is in line with that of my father, which will become apparent shortly. I wish I had a photograph of my father, but, unfortunately, my father did not have any pictures of himself on display. Most likely, he viewed photography as an attribute of the Babylonian way of life.

My father passionately embraced the Rastafarian doctrine, and it became his way of life. Besides adhering to his Rastafarian doctrine, he was a carpenter by trade and also a farmer. He planted vegetables and other crops that he used

---

3 According to the Religion Facts website (http://www.religionfacts.com), the movement of Rastafarianism or Rastafari developed in the slums of Kingston, Jamaica, in the 1920s. In an environment of great poverty, depression, racism, and class discrimination, the Rasta message of black pride, freedom from oppression, and the hope of return to the African homeland was gratefully received. Rastafarians' core belief is that Humans are temples of Jah and that God is Jah, who became incarnate in Jesus (who was black) and Haile Selassie. A number of the Rastafarian practices include the wearing of dreadlocks and abstinence from most or all forms of meat, artificial foods, and alcohol. The use of marijuana plays a significant role in religious rituals and medicinal purposes.

to feed his family. His carpentry profession provided the necessary financial support for the family. He cultivated most of the food we consumed. His philosophy was for us to "eat what we grow and grow what we eat." Very seldom did my father purchase any food from the grocery shops or the local markets. He told us that the crops that are cultivated by others are contaminated with fertilizer, pesticides, and other harmful chemicals. Based on what I know now, I would conclude that my father was one of the first Rastafarians to pioneer the art of organic cultivation.

Although my father was a Rastafarian and adhered to the Rastafarian doctrine, he seemed to have made an exception as it related to chickens and other livestock. He, at least for a while, reared a few goats, rabbits, and chickens, which he sold to the residents of the community. He did not rear pigs because he believed that pigs are possessed demons and not fit for human consumption. In addition to my father's farming, carpentry, chicken, and livestock rearing, he cultivated marijuana and lots of it!

Our Rastafarian diet did not include any meat or salt. My father stated that salt is a form of harlot and should not be eaten. This was one of the reasons why he did not purchase any baked, cooked, or processed foods or beverages. Even throughout the very rare times when he would partake of food that was prepared by one of his friends or brethren, he would enquire if the food had any salt in it. His exact words were, "Iah man, di I nuh put no harlot in a di I food?" ("Did you put any salt in the meal?") My father would go to great lengths to make sure that there was absolutely no salt (or harlot, as he claimed) in any of the food or beverages he consumed. Concerning meat, my

Chapter 1

father did not have to enquire because all of his friends knew quite well that he did not eat meat.

So what was this harlot my father kept referring to throughout many of his conversations? After a little research, I found out that my father was referring to Revelation 17:5. This scripture verse states, "And upon her forehead was a name written, mystery, Babylon the great, the mother of harlots and abominations of the earth" (KJV). My father also stated that Lot's wife was a harlot who had become a pillar of salt when she looked back at Sodom and Gomorrah while they were being consumed by fire (related in the book of Genesis). These biblical references are two of the reasons my father did not consume any salt.

Looking back, I would conclude that my father was a bit hypocritical (at least for a period). Although we did not consume meat, my father reared chickens and livestock for human consumption. However, he ceased livestock rearing when a rare form of disease wiped out his entire chicken farm. My father was convinced that this was a sign from Jah informing him that it was not a worthy practice to rear birds and other livestock for human consumption.

A typical day's activity started with the family spending anywhere from three to four hours on the farm. After we were through with the farming chores, my father harvested enough food and marijuana for the day's meals and smoking ritual. My sisters prepared breakfast for the family. After we were through with breakfast, my father rolled marijuana spliffs for us to smoke. Smoking marijuana several times per day was a sacred ritual that we practiced. According to my father, smoking marijuana was a form of worship and a means by which we gave thanks and praises unto the Most High Jah.

In addition to his farming, my father worked as a carpenter for Mr. Manboard, who was a wealthy (relatively speaking) farmer and business entrepreneur from the district of Darliston, Westmoreland. After we were through with the marijuana smoking ritual, my father left us at home and went to his carpentry work at Mr. Manboard's lumberyard and machine shop. Sometimes my brother and I would accompany our father to his workplace. On the days when he did not work at Mr. Manboard's lumberyard and machine shop, we would spend anywhere from six to eight hours on the farm. None of us (my sisters, my brother, or I) was allowed to attend school. Attending school was totally forbidden because our father stated that it was a form of Babylonian indoctrination. Overall, that was the lifestyle we had.

I am unable to recall how long this lifestyle lasted because, throughout such time, I had no real concept regarding minutes, hours, days, weeks, months, or years. All I knew back then was sunrise and sunset.

The Unforgettable Raid

This lifestyle came to an abrupt end for us (the children) when, one day, a number of police officers raided our home and took us away. After reading my file some thirty-four years later, I found out that this incident took place on August 13, 1975, which was a month and five days after my seventh birthday. As for the how, I remembered most of it because the images are still plastered in my mind to this very day.

It was a bright and sunny morning when we, except for my father, were at home when all of a sudden, two police

Chapter 1

officers magically appeared before us. Apparently, there were others, but I only witnessed the two who approached us. My father was at one of his plantations that were located within proximity to the house. The police officers shouted at him and demanded that he report to them right away. The minute my father showed up, they handcuffed him and started slapping him repeatedly with the blades of their machetes. Immediately we started screaming, hoping that the police would stop hitting our father. However, our crying and screaming did not deter them. After witnessing what was being done to our father, we ran into the house and hid underneath the bed. I really thought that the police officers were going to kill us. At the time, this was how it came across because the machetes that the police used to hit my father were much longer, thicker, and heavier than your everyday garden machetes; thus, the reason for his injuries that contributed to his suffering and, eventually, his death.

As a child, and more so throughout the writing of this incident, I found myself searching for motives as to what could have triggered such an unwarranted response by the police officers. After consulting with my sister, Paulette, she told me that on the day of the incident, one of the police officers had yelled at our father in a crude and derogatory manner and demanded that he report to them immediately. Instead of heeding their command with a sense of urgency, my father had told the police officers that he was on his way and would be there shortly. Although not a justification for their actions, presumably the police officers took offense with my father's demeanor and resorted to hitting him repeatedly with their machetes. Or it could be what they had intended to do regardless of his demeanor.

While we were there tucked away under the bed, we heard the door open, followed by footsteps coming toward us. We lay there quietly, hoping not to be seen by the person who had come into the room. However, moments later, one of the police officers peeked under the bed and shouted in a rather loud and crude manner, "Unnu Rasta pickney, come fram unda di bed!" ("You Rasta children, get out from underneath the bed.") We refused to heed his command, so he reached under the bed and dragged us out like animals. We were terrified! As for me, I thought the police officers had killed my father, and it was now our turn. After the policeman was through rounding us up like animals, he escorted us down the pathway that led to the main road.

While we were walking down the pathway, the curious neighbors came out of their homes to witness the drama unfold. After we reached the main road, the police officer placed us into one of the vehicles. I remember seeing the police going back and forth, carrying many large bales of marijuana, and stacking them in the vehicles, including the one we were in. I kept looking around for my father, but I did not see him anywhere. Just by observing the police officers going back and forth with the bales of marijuana, I concluded that they had finally gotten what they had come for.

After the jeep that we were in was filled from floor to ceiling with marijuana, two of the officers climbed into the vehicle and drove off with us. I had no idea where they were taking us. Moreover, the driving experience was very uncomfortable. From what I could recall, this was the first time that I had ridden in a motor vehicle. For reasons unknown to me, my father never allowed

Chapter 1

us to travel in any motor vehicle. We "footed it" everywhere we went, no matter the occasion or distance. As it relates to the "going green" initiative, we did not just talk the talk, we literally walked the walk. Nonetheless, this turned out to be the most unpleasant motor vehicle experience I ever had! The vehicle felt as though it were going up and down instead of moving forward. I started experiencing nausea and, eventually, I threw up. The police officers were not happy when they found out that I was throwing up inside the vehicle. At one point they instructed my sister to place my head outside the window. That only made matters worse. The up-and-down motion transformed into a circular motion. The vehicle felt as though it were going around in one giant circle.

Shortly after that, the policeman stopped the vehicle, got out, and went across the street to a local grocery shop. Moments later, he returned with a newspaper, gave it to my sister, and told her to stuff it between my shirt and my chest. At the time, I had no clue what this was for. I found out later that this is a common Jamaican practice for ridding a person of nausea or motion sickness. Even to this day, I am still not sure if it has any scientific truth to it. Sense or nonsense, after a short while I stopped throwing up. However, I did continue to experience the weird up-and-down motion of the vehicle. Most likely, this is a normal occurrence for people who suffer from motion sickness. In hindsight, seeing that this was a Toyota vehicle, I should have said, "Come on, Toyota! Let's go places!" In Toyota's defense, any vehicle with that much marijuana on board would undoubtedly exhibit erratic behaviors.

I was relieved when we finally made our first stop at the police station. When the vehicle came to a stop, one of the police officers escorted us into the building and placed us in a holding area that was located just outside the main prison block. I could see and hear the prisoners through the metal bars shouting and cursing whenever the police officers walked by the prison cells. By this time, several hours had gone by and we had not gotten anything to eat or drink. Later that afternoon, a female police officer came into the holding area and offered each of us a small bun and a soft drink. We ate the bun, but we did not drink the soda pop because our father forbade us to consume any bottled beverage. He stated that bottled beverages, especially alcohol, represent the Babylonian way of life that is designated for drunkards and harlots.

Later that evening, one of the police officers came into the holding area and took my brother and me away, leaving our sisters, Pauline and Paulette, behind. As my brother and I were being taken away, a lonely feeling came over me. At that moment, the thought of never being able to see my sisters again was devastating. It was one of those lonely feelings that are not easily expressed with words. My sisters had assumed the role of a mother regarding my brother and me. Therefore, being separated from them for the first time did cause me much emotional grief. Moreover, at such a young age, I did not have the mental capacity to understand the things that were happening to us. I could only surmise that my brother had the same or similar experience.

That day, my brother and I found ourselves being escorted to different areas of the building. Most likely, this constant movement was necessary for us to complete the transfer process. After a lengthy back-and-forth process, one of the police officers asked us (more like beckoned to

Chapter 1

us) to accompany him. He took us outside, placed us in one of the police vehicles, and told us that we were being taken to a home.

Now that my brother and I were getting ready to be shuttled off into the unknown, it is time to find out what had become of my father and my sisters. Many years later, Paulette told me that Mr. Manboard (my father's employer) had posted bail for our father. Things did not go as well for my sisters because when the police officers took them to an orphanage, the person in charge would not accept them when she found out that they were Rastafarians. According to Paulette, when the woman discovered that they were Rastafarian (Rasta), in a rather frightening tone she said, "Laud Jeezas! A whey unnu a guh wid dem deh Rasta pickney deh?" ("Lord Jesus! Where are you officers going with those two Rasta children?") Apparently, they had recently gone through a not-so-pleasant experience with a Rastafarian parent and did not want to go through another encounter. After several unsuccessful attempts to find a home for my sisters, the police officers took them back to the Savanna-la-Mar police station where they spent the night. Having no other viable option, the police returned my sisters to our father's care.

Now that we know what happened to my father and my sisters, it's time to find out what happened to my brother and me. While we were sitting in the vehicle, two police officers came out of the building with three other boys, who appeared to be much older than we were, and placed them in the vehicle with us. Finally, after several back-and-forth, here-and-there movements among different areas of the building, two officers came into the vehicle and drove off with us deeper into the unknown. After a long, bumpy, and yes, once again awful, up-and-down ride (this time I did not throw up), we made our first stop at this juvenile facility, which is known as Copse Juvenile Correctional institution/Copse Detention Center/Copse Place of Safety for boys. The police dropped off the three older boys at this institution and then drove off, taking us even further into the unknown. I learned quite early that Copse is one of the juvenile institutions feared by all boys who find themselves in the foster care system. This is also the case with minors (male) who find themselves on the wrong side of the law.

CHAPTER 2

LIFE AT THE ORPHANAGE

After enduring another bumpy, up-and-down, roller-coaster-like ride, the police officers made a second stop at another place, which turned out to be the Garland Hall Memorial Children's Home.[4] As soon as the vehicle entered the parking lot and came to a stop, I looked out the window and saw a big black dog running toward the vehicle. The dog was barking ferociously as if we were not welcome there. Or it could be that the dog was not fond of having Rastafarians on the property. Nevertheless, after we sat in the vehicle for a couple of minutes, a woman came onto the verandah and yelled at the dog. "Peps!" she said, and immediately the dog ran off to the back of the build-

---

[4] The Garland Hall Memorial Children's Home/orphanage is located in Anchovy, St. James, Jamaica. It is operated by the Jamaican Women's Baptist Federation. The orphanage is named after Elizabeth Garland Hall, who was a Baptist missionary and the founder of the Jamaican Women's Baptist Federation. (Hall, Elizabeth (Garland)). It provides accommodation for up to thirty children between the ages of nine and thirteen, except for a small number who could either be younger (as it was in my case) or older. Most of the children reside at the orphanage for several years, however, a number of them could end up spending their entire childhoods there.
https://dacb.org/stories/democratic-republic-of-congo/hall-elizabeth/

Chapter 2

ing. Now that I have had some time to think about this experience, I am not sure whether the woman yelled Peps or Pepsi. Okay, she said Peps, but I simply could not resist the thought. Anyway, after the dog had gone, one of the police officers opened the door and signaled to my brother and me to come out of the vehicle. We did accordingly and accompanied him up the stairs and onto the verandah.

As soon as the woman noticed that my brother and I were Rastafarians, she uttered something to the effect of, "A two Rasta pickney dem, an dem need fi trim." What she meant was, "It is two Rasta children, and they are in need of a haircut." Due to my communication deficit as a result of not being allowed to attend school, I could not understand much of her conversation. However, she was emphasizing the need for us to have our hair cut as soon as possible. Based on her initial reaction, it is obvious that she was not about to condone any Rastafarian lifestyle at the orphanage. After the police and the director were through conversing, they bid each other goodbye and the police officers drove away, leaving us behind.

Although the woman had not introduced herself to us officially, that did not matter because we overheard the children addressing her as Auntie and we did likewise. What was even more surprising was the fact that it was not until the writing of my autobiography, some thirty years later, before I found out that Auntie was the director of the orphanage and that her real name was Edna Harty. Seeing that the children addressed her as Auntie, I will continue to refer to her as such from this point forward.

Shortly after that, Auntie beckoned to a woman (the dorm monitor) and told her to accompany us to the bathroom and see to it that we showered and dressed in clean clothes. However, we were unable to shower because we had no knowledge of what to do. This was our first attempt at bathing without the aid of a bucket or a washtub. After noticing that we had no clue of what to do, the woman came in and operated the taps for us. Besides, this was our first time being introduced to a flushable toilet. After we were through with our showers, the woman escorted us to the dormitory, presented us with clean clothes, and assigned us to our beds.

Although we were quite hungry, unfortunately, we did not get anything to eat that evening. I also found out that whenever a child was taken to the orphanage outside assigned mealtimes, he or she would have no choice but to wait until the next meal was served. We arrived after supper was served, so we had to endure a long and hungry night because breakfast was the next scheduled meal. This reminds me of a popular Jamaican phrase, "If you show up late, then dawg nyam yuh suppa." Which is to say, "If you are not present when meals are served, then there will be no food left for you." For all we know, it could have been Peps who ate our supper. Speaking of Peps, do you remember the ferocious barking he was doing when we first arrived? Well, all that was just for show, because we happened to cross path several times after that, but he was as quiet as a lamb. I mean, he did not even growl once.

So there we were dressed in our pajamas, lying in our warm and cozy beds, with not much to do but try and anticipate the unexpected. Instead of enjoying a good night's sleep, we found ourselves being bombarded with many questions from the other boys. I did not answer any of the questions directed at me because I was not sure what they were saying. My brother tried to interact with them,

Chapter 2

but they kept laughing because of his communication defecit. He was communicating in the manner that our father had taught us. That is, he was substituting the words "me" and "my" with the word "I." For example, when they enquired our names, my brother responded by saying, "I an I a Son an Iah." Son and Iah are the Rastafarian names that our father had assigned to us. That night the older boys kept talking to my brother because they just could not get enough of his "I an I" dialect.

As for me, I kept quiet and did not even attempt to say a single "I." Not only that, but I felt a real sense of loneliness because this was the first time that I could recall being separated from my father and sisters. However, knowing that my brother was there with me did ease my emotional pain. This new environment and lifestyle were vastly different from what I had been accustomed to while living with my father. Everything about this place kept reminding me that I did not belong there.

As the night progressed, I could hear the other boys talking and laughing among themselves. I presumed it was outside the norm for the orphanage to entertain Rastafarian children. Actually, for the entire time I spent at the orphanage, I never witnessed another Rastafarian child being taken there. That night I had a difficult time sleeping due to anxiety and the dormitory drama that was unfolding. Not only that, but I was quite hungry too. However, I finally got a little nap into the wee hours of the morning.

First Day Away from Home

The next morning I woke up very early, just as the sunlight began to pierce through the window curtains. Everyone

Life at the Orphanage

was sound asleep. As I lay there, many voices kept buzzing around in my head. I could not help but wonder what was going to happen next. I was hoping that my father and my sisters would come and take us away from this place. Shortly after that, my brother woke up and we went outside and sat down under a June plum tree that was located at the back of the building. I am not sure what we talked about while we were there sitting under the tree. However, our tranquility was interrupted by a distinct smell that started filling the air. This rather odd smell was very overpowering. I felt as if I were about to throw up.

Later that morning, I saw the other children coming out from their respective dorms. We did not have a clue what to expect, so we remained seated under the tree. Shortly after that, I heard a rather strange sound that lasted for a couple of seconds. At the time, I had no idea what was making that strange sound. However, I learned that the instrument was a bell, and it was used to alert the children that their meals were served. Immediately after the children heard the bell, they took off running in one general direction. At the time, my brother and I had no idea why the children were running in that particular direction. However, we learned that once you hear the ringing of the bell, you need to get to the dining room right away so that your meal does not end up becoming someone else's second helping. Anyway, within a couple of seconds, we were the only two children left outside. After approximately thirty minutes, I saw the children coming out of the dining room. They were laughing and talking among themselves. I guess they were quite happy to have enjoyed their first meal of the day. Wow! It took just one meal for a child to express that much joy! I wish

Chapter 2

those who had contributed to such a moment had been there to witness it.

Apparently, a number of the boys had noticed that there were two unclaimed meals left on the dining table because they came over to where we were and said, "Bwoy, unnu naa guh nyam unnu food?" ("Aren't you guys going to eat your meals?") With a bit of persuasion, my brother and I got up and accompanied one of the boys to the dining room. However, as we approached the dining room, we were greeted by an overpowering smell. I can still picture the expression on my brother's face. It was one of those "What the heck!" type of expressions. Anyway, the minute we entered the dining room and saw rather odd-looking, chopped-up, smelly things on our plates, we ran out of the dining room as fast as we could. We definitely did not want to have anything to do with what we had seen on our plates.

We knew right away that the red-looking things were dead animal flesh. However, the thing that grossed us out the most was the red, blood-like liquid that was splattered all over the plates. Later we found out that the chopped-up meat and the red liquid we saw on our plates had been sausage and ketchup, not meat drenched in blood as we had originally thought. My father used some of the most graphic descriptions—such as dead carcass, rotten flesh, and dead harlot—when referring to meat and the consumption of meat. He also considered anyone who consumed meat as Jancro/jangkro (John Crow), which are commonly used Jamaican Patois labels for vulture or scavenger. My father's graphic depiction of meat would undoubtedly turn a person's mind against the consumption of meat. We just could not understand why they were feeding the children with animal flesh and blood!

Life at the Orphanage

For the rest of the day, we were traumatized by what we had witnessed. The image of flesh and blood was etched in my mind for a long time, and I believe this was true for my brother as well. If I had anything left in my stomach that morning, it would certainly have come pouring out. My brother and I refused to consume any meals that were prepared in a place that was contaminated with flesh and blood. We did not even take a sip of the hot beverage (tea) that was on the table. In fact, we ran out of the dining room and did not return for the rest of the day.

While my brother and I were in the backyard, a number of the boys came by and kept asking us permission to have our meals. They did not know our names, but that did not deter them. They were quite eager to have our meals, so one of the boys addressed us by saying, "Nyah bwoy, gimme yuh food." ("Nyah boy, give me your food.") That triggered a chain reaction, and all the boys who were present started addressing us in such a manner. A number of them came up to me and kept shouting, "Red Nyah bwoy, gimme yuh food." ("Red Nyah boy, give me your food.") "A mi fuss ax yuh." ("It was me who asked first.")

Similarly, they addressed my brother, except they addressed him as Black Nyah. That morning I witnessed one mass confusion because several of the boys were jockeying for our meals. To further complicate the matter, my brother and I were lacking the desired level of communication skills to respond appropriately. Therefore, we had no idea who had asked first or who should have been the ones to have our meals. I guess we did not care to know either.

Why did they address us as Black Nyah and Red Nyah? Nyah is another label used to address Rastafarians. Seeing that my brother and I are of dark and light complexions,

Chapter 2

respectively, the children used complexion to differentiate between us. From that point forward, everyone, including the staff members, addressed us as Black Nyah and Red Nyah, respectively.

Cutting Off Our Locks

Later that morning, my brother and I were approached by a man who informed us that he had been authorized to take us to the barber. He said something to the effect of, "Yuh two Rasta bwoy, cum trim unno head." ("You two Rastafarian boys, come and get your hair cut.") He took us down a dirt path and then onto a rather odd-looking thing that appeared to be a giant ladder. This odd-looking thing reminded me of a ladder because my father is a carpenter and had several ladders of different lengths or heights depending on the position (horizontal or vertical). However, this was the first time that I had ever seen such a long ladder. Okay, it's time for me to break the suspense and let you know that the odd-looking thing I was fascinated with was just an old-fashioned railroad track. We walked along the railroad track or, as it was in my case, the long ladder until we arrived at a little barbershop that was located within proximity to the orphanage.

My brother was the first to be escorted into the barber's chair. He sat quietly and got his hair cut like a true gentleman. When it was my turn, "all hell broke loose." I did not want to have my hair (locks) cut at all! I simply was not going down to Babylon without a fight. However, they got the better of me when a man picked me up off the floor and placed me in the barber chair. Even when I was forced to sit in the barber chair, I remember putting up a real fight, kicking and screaming. None of that saved me because when it was all over, I left the barbershop with absolutely no locks left on my head. After all those years of being a Rastafarian, within a matter of minutes, we were reduced to total baldheads. Long after the incident, the man (Mr. Palmer) who had taken us to the barber told me that I had put up a real fight each time the barber cut off a portion of my locks. He said, "For the entire duration, you kept repeating, 'Di I locks burning.'" ("My locks are burning.") I am not sure why I thought my locks were burning. Probably it had something to do with my father's strict Rastafarian doctrine concerning our locks. Our father had specifically told us not to let anyone put any form of Babylonian harlots in our locks. That is, never let anyone cut or comb our hair.

After the haircut drama was over, my brother and I were escorted back to the orphanage. Upon arrival, the children were quite curious to see what we looked like without our locks. Although we were now baldheaded, that did not stop them from addressing us as Black Nyah and Red Nyah. Later that afternoon, the bell rang again. This time it was signaling to the children that dinner was served. The yard was quiet once again because the children had gone into the dining room to enjoy their meal. However, based on our first traumatic dining room experience, my brother and I decided to stay put. We did not go anywhere near the dining room for the rest of the day. The graphic image of flesh and blood was still fresh in my mind, and I could see that it was the same for my brother as well.

The peace and tranquility did not last for long because after the children were through with their meals, a number of the boys ran toward us like a pack of hungry

Chapter 2

wolves, with each repeating the Black Nyah, Red Nyah, may I have your meal drama all over again. I am not sure if we gave them permission or not, but once again they took off running toward the dining room, arguing among themselves. Each one was trying to convince the other that he was the first to ask and he was the one permitted to have our meals.

After the dinner "feast" was over, a number of the children engaged in leisure activities, while the others were busy performing their afternoon chores. The afternoon chores included washing the paved walkways and removing the leaves and other debris from the surrounding areas. My brother and I did not take part in any of the activities, we just observed from the sideline. After they were through, the boys took turns showering with the aid of a standpipe that was located at the back of the building, while the girls showered in the bathroom. I guess the boys did not care about privacy. After they were through showering and dressed in clean attire, I heard the bell ring once more. This time it was signaling to the children that supper was served. Once again, my brother and I did not budge. That day we did not eat any breakfast, dinner, or supper. Although we were quite hungry, we refused to eat our meals because our father had explicitly told us not to conform to the Babylonian lifestyle.

After supper, one of the older boys told us that we needed to go and take a shower. We used the bathroom instead of the standpipe that was located in the open yard. Yes, it was the same bathroom with strange gadgets such as taps and a flushable toilet. After we were through showering, we went directly to bed because we were hungry and simply did not have the energy to entertain any conversation. Despite the biological disorder (hunger, stress, and distress), I slept quite well that night.

The second day's routine was pretty much the same as the first. That is, we got up, went outside, and sat down under the June plum tree located at the back of the building. The bell rang, and the children hurried off to the dining room. After they were through eating, a number of the boys started competing for the rights to have our Babylonian meals. Once again, after enduring another day's hunger, we finally retired to bed.

The third day, my brother and I got up very early and, instead of sitting down under a tree as we had done the previous two days, we went into the little carpenter's workshop located behind the kitchen. By this time, everyone, including the cooks, had found out that my brother and I had not eaten anything in two days. I remember one of the cooks (I do believe it was Ms. Sarah) prepared and served us a bowl of ital rice. The word ital in the Rastafarian vocabulary means fresh, not having any salt, or, as it was in my father's case, meals not having any meat or salt but having quite a lot of marijuana. I remembered eating every grain of rice that was in the little bowl.

I do not recall how many days we were fed in this manner, however, what I do know is that it came to an end one day when the cooks told us that we would not be receiving any more ital rice. I could see that this was not an easy decision for the cooks because they were looking quite sad. With that in mind, we went back to the workshop and sat there for the duration. Later that evening, we showered and then retired to bed. Once again, it was another long twenty-four hours without any food. Just to be clear, this hunger was self-inflicted because we were provided with three meals.

Chapter 2

We were the ones who refused to conform to the norms of the orphanage.

One day, while my brother and I were sitting down in the open yard, we heard familiar sounds coming from the workshop. These sounds (saw, hammer, plane) were accustomed to our ears because we used to accompany our father to his carpentry workshop. If you recall, this was one of our daily routines because we were not allowed to attend school. So, with that in mind, we got up immediately and ran into the workshop, hoping to see our father. To our dismay, we did not see our father, but instead, we saw a man busy at work making and repairing furniture. The irony of this whole experience was the fact that this man was also a Rastafarian. The only difference between him and my father was that he wore a tam or beanie. His likeness and job profession were the closest we had gotten to being reunited with our father. We sat there and watched him as he toiled away at his job. My brother and I spent the rest of the morning in the workshop. Later that afternoon, the man packed away his tools and left. Once again, it was yet another day without food for my brother and me.

The following day my brother and I got up early and went into the workshop, but the man was not there. Despite not seeing him, we sat in the workshop hoping that he would eventually show up. Shortly after that, he came into the workshop and said something to the effect of, "Yout man, unnu deh yah again?" ("You guys are here again?") I am not sure what our response was, but I remember later that afternoon he said, "Yout man, unnu hungry?" ("Guys, are you hungry?") We replied, "Yes." Then he took two small bowls from his bag and served us rice and callaloo.

Callaloo is a green, leafy vegetable similar to spinach. Before we consumed any of it, my brother told him that we only eat ital food. With no hesitation, he replied, "Yeh man, dis yah a ital food man!" ("Yes, this is ital food!") After taking the first bite, I knew right then and there that the man was speaking the truth because it tasted just like my father's meals. I remember the man told us to eat quickly, but he did not give us any indication as to why.

Later I found out that he had done so because he did not want any of the other children to find out that he was providing us with food. At the time, I was not sure why he went out of his way to provide us with ital meals. I could only surmise that it was one of the workers (Ms. Sarah or Ms. Sylvia) who had pleaded our case to him. My brother and I developed a bond with him because he reminded us of our father. We were very happy to be in his company. Well, I must confess that we were mostly there for his ital food. The man provided us with hot meals for a couple of days. I am unable to say exactly how many days, because I was not keeping track. Nonetheless, our joy turned to sorrow when, one day, the man told us that he was not allowed to provide us with any more food. We were also forbidden from hanging out with him in the workshop.

Here is what actually happened: The director (Auntie) told the staff members, including the carpenter, not to provide us with any more ital or Rastafarian meals because her goal was to rid us of the Rastafarian doctrine. On the one hand, I do understand the concerns and empathy displayed by the employees. However, on the other, I do understand Auntie's rationale. In fact, getting us through the transition process was Auntie's primary responsibility. Therefore, if she were unable to rid us of the Rastafarian doctrine, then

Chapter 2

it would only complicate matters in such regard. Probably Auntie's rationale was that as soon as the hunger became unbearable, we would have no other choice but to eat the food that was made available to us.

So there went our only source of ital food. Now we were left with only two choices: Defy our father's strict Rastafarian mandate and eat the Babylonian food, or refuse to conform and die of starvation. With that said, I am not sure how many more hunger-days we endured.

After the hunger became unbearable, I decided that I was going to run away from the orphanage. At first, running away was just a mere thought. However, my runaway idea was manifested one day when a little idea popped into my head while I was sitting on a rock located at the front of the building overlooking the railroad track and the main road.

As I sat there observing the motor vehicles and pedestrians go by, suddenly it dawned on me that if I were to only follow the road, it would eventually take me to my father's home. In hindsight, this was definitely not a well-thought-out idea, but at the time, this option seemed a whole lot better than staying at an orphanage that did not cater to Rastafarians. For some unknown reason, I did not mention my secret runaway plan to my brother. Probably I was worried that he would try and convince me that it was not a good idea.

The following night, when everyone, including my brother, had retreated to bed, I took matters into my own hands, snuck out of the dorm, ran off the property, and finally took off running down the road. I did not have the slightest clue where I was going because it was quite dark except for the one or two streetlights and the faint lights

Life at the Orphanage

illuminating from inside the homes. I kept on running until I came to a place (bar or pub) where several men were congregated. I knew that I needed some help locating my father, so I decided to stop and ask for directions. However, running into the bar and asking for directions was not an action I wanted to take.

I remember standing on the outside for a good while, contemplating what to do. On the one hand, I knew I needed help locating my father. While on the other hand, I was very much afraid of being taken back to the orphanage. Have you heard the stereotype that a man would rather be lost than ask for directions? I am here to debunk that theory because I went into the bar, walked directly over to where one of the guys was sitting, and in an eloquent manner, asked him for directions to my father's house.

Well, it was not in such a bold and forthright manner. Actually, I walked gingerly into the bar and used the "I an I" dialect to mumble a few words to the man who was sitting closest to the door. After I was through, the man turned his head, looked at me, and said, "A wah yuh faada name?" ("What is your father's name?") I told him, "Iah." He turned around, looked at me, and said, "Iah! Mi nuh know nobady name Iah." ("Iah! I do not know of anyone by that name.") He then asked me several questions for which I had few or no answers. I believe that, based on my communication deficit, the man detected that I was attempting to run away from the orphanage.

Like an experienced lawyer, the man concluded the interrogation process by saying, "No further questions, your honor." Not really in that manner, but the man did end the conversation abruptly and told me to have a seat and wait until he was through with his beer or whatever

Chapter 2

Babylonian drink he was having. I was very thirsty, so I asked him for some water. With no hesitation, he picked up a glass that was filled with water, or what appeared to be water, and gave it to me. The minute I took the first gulp, I knew that what I was drinking was definitely not water. Let me emphasize, ladies and gentlemen, that was the most unpleasant liquid I had ever tasted. Despite the unpleasant taste, I drank it to the very last drop. Probably the thirst and the hunger suppressed the bad taste to the point that I convinced myself that I was drinking water. Anyway, long after the incident, I found out that the man had given me a tall glass of diluted, over-proofed Jamaican rum instead of a glass of water. I am not sure if this was an honest mistake or he was pulling a practical joke on me.

Nonetheless, after I was through drinking the glass of diluted rum (Babylonian drink as per my father), the man assured me that he would take me home to my father. Upon hearing such comforting words, I was very happy because, in my mind, I was finally going home to be with my father. However, after sitting there for a while, I started feeling a bit light-headed, and it appeared as though everything was moving away from me ever so slowly. At the time, I had no idea what was happening or why I was experiencing such a strange feeling. However, despite the strange feeling, my main concern was not to squander this golden going-home opportunity.

After the man was through drinking and chatting with his friends (or brethren as we say in Jamaica), he took me to his car, placed me inside, climbed in, and drove off. Before I could get too comfortable, the car came to a stop. Although I was not in my right frame of mind (due to the alcohol I had consumed), nor had

Life at the Orphanage

I any knowledge concerning speed, distance, or time, something about this going-home trip just did not feel right. In other words, my instinct told me that there was no way that we could have made it to my father's home that quickly. Sure enough, the minute I looked out the car window I noticed that the place looked quite familiar. That was when it dawned on me that I had been tricked, bamboozled, and fooled into thinking that I was on my way home to be reunited with my father. Instead, the man had taken me right back to the orphanage.

From the very start, there were two major flaws with my decision to run away from the orphanage. First, I should have included my brother in my runaway plan. And second, I should not have stopped and asked for directions. As for the second mishap, I will go back to being a typical man who refuses to stop and ask for directions!

Anyway, Auntie thanked the man, then she escorted me to the dorm and told me to go to bed. From that point forward, I did not have a clue about what was happening. In the morning, I overheard the other boys laughing and talking among themselves. They told me that I had been as drunk as a bat and saying all sorts of crazy things. If I had a problem communicating while I was sober, then one could only imagine what it was like when I was drunk. At least my behavior had confirmed my hypothesis that the man at the bar had indeed given me a glass of diluted alcohol beverage, most likely Jamaican overproof rum. And, in the words of an angry British, "No wonder the bloody thing tasted so bad!"

After enduring such a disappointing and, yes, embarrassing experience, that was the first and the last time that I ran away from the orphanage. Even to this very day, I am still trying to figure out why Mr. Wray and his Nephew (a

Chapter 2

popular brand of Jamaican rum) are so proud of something that tastes so bad. However, I must confess that I do like a little rum in my Jamaican sorrel drink and, most of all, my favorite Jamaican rum cake. Yummy!

Okay, let's stop salivating and get back to the ordeal at the orphanage. I do believe that the following day one of the older boys (not sure which one) gave my brother and me two slices of bread each and told us that it was ital bread (fresh, no salt). We took the bread and ate it quickly. Still terrified by our first dining room experience, each day we would sit outside and wait for one of the boys to bring us the bread and the hot Milo (chocolate) beverage from our breakfast and supper meals. I guess they saw how hungry we were and realized that our meals should no longer be their second helpings. However, we gave them permission to have our dinners because they contained meat.

I am not sure how long this episode lasted but, from what I remember, my brother and I started joining the other children for breakfast and supper. However, we would only eat the bread and drink the hot Milo beverage. I can assure you that this was certainly a difficult transition for us! Nonetheless, we had to conform to our new environment.

This slow progression went on for a while until we started eating bread with cheese, jam/jelly, or butter. Although it took us a while, it came to a point where we finally started eating meat. However, I refused to eat meals that contained fish, due to the raw odor. After many days of experiencing nausea-like feelings, I finally was able to eat my meals with few or no side effects. The slow and painful progression was about the same for my brother. After a while, we were fully acclimated to the orphanage life and society in general. Or, as my father would say, the Babylonian way of life. I mean,

Life at the Orphanage

we were eating, talking, and walking like Babylonians. Okay, I am not sure if we were walking like Babylonians. Nonetheless, we were speaking without using the "I an I" dialect and were consuming our regular meals (with meat and salt) with no problem. As the old saying goes, "When in Rome do as the Romans do." Or, as it was in our case, "When in Babylon do as the Babylonians do."

Besides, we were no longer antisocial. That is, we participated in the daily activities, with one exception: we were not allowed to leave the orphanage. Only a small number of children, including the mentally and or physically challenged, were exempted from attending school or church. I could only surmise that it was due to our extreme literacy deficit why my brother and I were not allowed to attend school.

One day we were surprised when we saw several strange people showed up at the orphanage. They brought a wide variety of snacks and gave them to the children, including my brother and me. I used the word strange because this was the first time George and I saw white/Caucasian people. Anyway, our curiosity did not last because we got used to them coming by the orphanage regularly. Most of the visitors were there to teach the children about Christianity. However, I noticed that the children were more interested in the meals and or tasty treats than they were about anything else. In hindsight, one would hope that my brother and I would never find ourselves going through such a painful transition again! Well, let's continue reading to see if that was the case.

Just as life at the orphanage became routine, it was abruptly interrupted when my brother and I were summoned to the front verandah. This section of the orphanage was

Chapter 2

one of the few areas that were off limits to the children, except on special occasions such as visitations, arrivals, and departures. Therefore, we knew right then and there that something out of the ordinary was about to happen. The minute we showed up, we were greeted by a representative from the Child Development Agency (CDA). After a short introduction, she asked us if we were happy to be at the orphanage. I am not sure what our response was. The one question I remember that we gave a resounding yes answer to, was when she asked us if we would like to go back home to live with our father. As for me, I was hoping that my father was there to take us home. I believe that it was the same expectation my brother had as well.

After hearing our enthusiastic response, the CDA officer told us about the wonderful promises our father had made regarding our well-being. One of those promises, or should I say commitments, was that he would allow us to attend school. She also told us that our sisters were home with our father and they were attending school as well. At the end of the conversation, she reminded us that our father was still rooted in the Rastafarian doctrine. That was old news for us because it was highly unlikely that our father would sacrifice his most sacred tradition to regain custody of his children. Irrespective of my father's Rastafarian doctrine, I was more than happy to be going home. However, after the CDA officer was through with her conversation, she said goodbye, went to her car, and drove off, leaving us behind. At the time, this did not make any sense to me because I thought that she had been there to take us home. Moreover, she left without telling us when she would return.

Life at the Orphanage

With that said, we had no other choice but to return to our daily routine at the orphanage. Well, the above statement does not paint an accurate picture of what was going on in my mind after being told that I would someday be reunited with our father. In fact, I woke up every day looking out for my father.

The Much-Anticipated Day Finally Arrives

One morning, just after we were through eating breakfast, my brother and I were summoned to take showers, get dressed, and go to the front verandah. Although we were not told explicitly why, nonetheless, we knew that it had something to do with both of us *"leaving"* the orphanage that day. I have emphasized the word leaving because it was not guaranteed that a child would leave the orphanage simply because the child was told to get dressed and sit on the verandah. In fact, I witnessed several children who got dressed and sat all day on the little bench located in the corner of the verandah but never got picked up. Despite the likelihood of us not leaving the orphanage that day, we both were very excited and hoped that the long-awaited day had finally arrived. Without any hesitation we showered (more like ran in and ran out of the bathroom), got dressed, and rushed to the verandah, hoping to see our father. To our dismay, our father was not there. In fact, there was no one there to greet us. Anyway, we sat on the bench and kept looking out, hoping that the next person coming up the driveway would be our father.

Before I proceed, I would like to provide you with a little more insight regarding the significance of the front verandah, at least from the children's perspective. From

Chapter 2

a practical point of view, the verandah was where a child was dropped off and picked up. In computer terms, it is similar to a staging area or a temporary buffer. For all my fellow computer geeks out there, the orphanage is like one big extract, transform, and load (ETL) process. For example, in the case of my brother and me, the process was as follows: **Extract**–take two Rastafarian children away from their parents and place them in an orphanage. **Transform**–rid them of the Rastafarian lifestyle by introducing them to the norms of society as depicted by the orphanage. **Load**–return them to their biological family or transfer them to a foster home.

There were times when the verandah, or the staging area, would turn out to be an embarrassing situation for the child or children who got dressed and sat there for hours, sometimes all day, and never got picked up by their biological or prospective adoptive or foster parents. For you to understand the psychological effect this can have on a child, I will share with you an incident that involved a little girl who got dressed and sat on the verandah all day but never got picked up.

I remember this girl, whose nickname was Cool Cat. We addressed her as such because she was so meager, she reminded us of the cat that is featured in the Desnoes and Geddes Limited (D&G) logo. Anyway, that particular day she got dressed and sat all day on the little wooden bench located in the corner of the front verandah, but never got picked up by anyone. Finally, late into the evening, she was summoned to the dorm and told to change into her regular, everyday orphanage attire. The disappointment overwhelmed her to the point that she could not hold back the tears. I mean, she cried for a very long time. The point

Life at the Orphanage

Front view of the Garland Hall Memorial Children's Home, taken in 2009. Left of the entrance was the designated staging area.

Front view of Garland Hall as it appeared in 2019.

Chapter 2

I am conveying is that it can turn out to be a very disappointing experience for the child who finds him- or herself sitting on the verandah for many hours only to be told that he or she is not leaving the orphanage that day.

However, this day turned out to be a lucky day for my brother and me. After sitting on the verandah for several hours, we saw a car coming up the driveway. The minute the car came to a stop, a woman came out. She hurried up the steps and onto the verandah. She introduced herself as a CDA officer and told us that she was there to take us home to our father. I was so happy to be leaving the orphanage! Therefore, it did not make a difference who was there to take me home. After the transfer process concluded, my brother and I bid goodbye to Auntie as we accompanied the CDA officer to the car. After we were all seated, the CDA officer bid one final goodbye to the director (Auntie), and we commenced our long journey home.

CHAPTER 3

THE ADVENTUROUS HOMECOMING

As we drove away from the orphanage, I was overwhelmed with a profound sense of joy and happiness. However, for some unknown reason, I found myself looking out the window, staring at the orphanage until it was no longer in sight. The Child Development Agency (CDA) officer was talking, but I did not hear much of what she was saying because of the excitement that was buzzing around in my mind. My brother did all the talking because all I was concerned about was the fact that we were finally on our way home. We drove for a good while until we made our first stop at a bustling marketplace located in Savanna-la-Mar, Westmoreland.

After arriving at the busy market, the CDA officer drove over to an area where several buses were parked. She stopped the car, opened the door, and beckoned to us to come on out. We did accordingly and followed her to where a big bus was parked. We, including the CDA officer, went on board and sat on one of the seats. I do not remember much of what she said. However, I distinctly

Chapter 3

remember she told us that the driver of the bus had promised to take us home to our father. Shortly after that, she got off the bus and waved one final goodbye as we gazed at her through the window. And that was the last time we saw or heard from her.

By this time it was late in the afternoon, and my brother and I were sitting in the parked bus witnessing the many events that were unfolding around us. I could see the people, the vehicles, the vendors, and the stray animals that were out and about roaming the busy streets and marketplace. Several of the street vendors came by the bus window and hollered out the names of the products they were selling. The most obnoxious of them were the peanut vendors. They kept on shouting, "Pee . . . nuts! Nuts! Nutsy!" Over and over, and over again! Occasionally, they would come inside the bus and walk up and down the aisle several times, asking each passenger if he or she would like to buy a bag of peanuts. As the day dragged on, I started feeling a bit hungry. Although the peanut vendors were quite obnoxious, I was very tempted to ask for a bag of peanuts. However, that was out of the question because neither my brother nor I had any money.

As the sun sets over the horizon, the hustle and bustle of the marketplace started to subside. This was an indication that the busy day's activities were coming to an end, and it would be only a matter of time before we were on our way home. Later in the evening, the driver started honking the horn to signal the vendors and passengers that the bus was getting ready to leave town. I could see the last-minute passengers running toward the bus. Several passengers did not get seats and had to stand for the duration of their journeys or wait until seats became available.

The Adventurous Homecoming

The bus was packed beyond capacity. There were just as many people standing as were sitting.

By this time, it was pitch dark because the sun was long gone beneath the horizon. Although there were very few street lights, the bus driver (or driva/jiva, as we say in Jamaica) was "full steam" ahead, navigating his way through the winding country road. I kept looking out the window but had no idea where I was or how long it would take before we arrived at our destination. Nonetheless, I was happy to be finally going home! In the words of Oleta Adams, it doesn't matter what road he takes or how many stops he makes, I don't care how late he gets there, just get there if he can. Okay, songwriting is surely not my hidden forte, so let me get back to the journey at hand.

There we were, observing as the driver navigated the bus through the dark, narrow, winding roads, making frequent stops for people to embark and disembark. Finally, after many stops, a man came over to where my brother and I were and told us to get ready because we were getting off at the next stop. By then it was very dark, so I had no clue where I was or, better yet, who was this person alerting us regarding our stop. I was so happy that even if a chimpanzee had approached me and told me that it had been assigned to take me home, I would have believed every word. I was not too concerned with the process because I knew that every stop meant that I was one stop closer to home. And that was evident because at the next stop, the man beckoned to us to accompany him off the bus.

The minute we go off the bus, we diverted off the main road onto a rocky, unpaved trail. Although it was quite dark, something about this trail was familiar. The man was walking briskly. Most likely, he had a mental picture of

Chapter 3

the pathway. My brother and I had to walk at a rapid pace to keep up. After walking for a while, we finally stopped at a little house that was located at the end of the trail. The man who escorted us started calling for my father. He yelled out, "Iah, Iah, Iah-man," several times. Iah was my father's Rastafarian name, which I was quite familiar with because it was my Rastafarian name as well. After several calls, I heard someone reply from inside the house. I was unable to see anyone because there were no lights. As a matter of fact, the only available lights were the ones being emitted by the fireflies (Jamaicans called them Peenie Wallies) that were glowing in the dark.

Shortly after that, a person came out of the house and shined a flashlight directly at us while, asking, "A who a call di I" ("Who is calling me?") The man who escorted us replied, "It's me, Ralph." Then he said, "Iah, me bring yuh two youtman dem, an dem de yasso wid mi." ("Iah, I brought your two sons home, and they are right here with me.") I detected that my father sounded a bit surprised, as if he had not been expecting us. Perhaps he had been expecting us but was unaware of the exact date of our arrival. Back in those days, very few Jamaicans had telephones. Therefore, most communications were done by word of mouth or by the post office. Moreover, my father considered electricity, phones, post offices, and other similar things to be associated with the Babylonian lifestyle. Therefore, the Child Development Agency had no way of communicating to him the exact date of our arrival.

The man and my father greeted each other and talked for a short while. Then they bid each other goodbye, and my father, brother, and I went inside the house. As soon as we were inside, my brother and I received a hearty welcome-home greeting from our sisters, Pauline and Paulette (or should I say I-line and I-lette). It was a wonderful experience to be home with my family again. After a brief welcome-home discussion, we retired to bed. The house had only two bedrooms, so my brother and I shared one of the rooms with our father, while our sisters occupied the other room. We were no strangers to this arrangement because this was the same accommodation we had before being taken to the orphanage.

Life with My Father and My Siblings

That night I remembered experiencing much anxiety. However, it was my father's constant moaning and groaning that kept us up most of the night. We inquired of our father the reason, and he reminded us of the severe beating that he had suffered at the hands of the police officers. His actual words were, "Di Babylon, dem mashup di I structure." ("The police officers caused injuries to my body.") Here is a reminder of what had happened: The day the police destroyed my father's marijuana plantation, they handcuffed him and then used their machetes to inflict severe blows to his body. My father also told me that even when he fell to the ground and was unable to get up, they resorted to kicking him repeatedly. This outright abuse was the cause of my father's internal bleeding. Although I was a child when this incident took place, I understood quite well that my father's pain and suffering were a direct result of the severe beating that had been inflicted on him by the rogue police officers. My father's health was never the same since that day. My brother and I had to forego many nights' sleep because our father would be up most of the night moaning from chronic

Chapter 3

pain. This dark past certainly brought back sad and painful memories as if it had happened yesterday. My father also compounded his physical ailment by refusing to seek medical attention or advice. He was deeply rooted in his Rastafarian doctrine. He believed that marijuana was the cure to all known ailments.

Our daily routine started out with my sisters preparing breakfast in the little outdoor kitchen that was located approximately twenty feet away from the house. While my sisters were busy preparing breakfast, my brother and I were given one of our father's stern "out of Babylon" lectures. He wanted to set the record straight. He reminded us to address him as Iah, not dad, daddy, or papa. He also reminded us not to use the words "me" or "my" in any of our conversation. The word "I" should be substituted for those words at all times. For example, if I wanted to say "This is for me, or this belongs to me," I would have to say, "This is for I, or this belongs to I."

He also reminded us of our Rastafarian names, which are Son and Iah. Not George and Desmond as per the CDA and the orphanage. However, I was surprised when I found out many years later that my Rastafarian name (Iah) was also recorded in my file by the CDA. Finally, our father reminded us that Pauline and Paulette should be addressed as I-line and I-lette, respectively. But wait! Why was it necessary that my sisters and me (I-line, I-lette, and Iah) had our names prefixed with the letter I, but it was not the same for my brother (Son)? Why not I-Son? Not only that, but seeing that my father had already taken ownership of the name Iah, then wouldn't it have been more appropriate if I were addressed as Iah Jr.? Just a couple of thoughts. In hindsight I am not sure why my father was subjecting

The Adventurous Homecoming

us to such a rigorous Rastafarian indoctrination. Maybe he thought that we had forgotten everything about the Rastafarian lifestyle. Later that morning, after my father was through with his lecturing, my sisters served breakfast. Okay, let's find out if my brother and I had received our regular Babylonian sausage, scrambled eggs, or shredded cheese. Well, I guess not! We were served the same old Rastafarian ital breakfast, which included roasted breadfruit, yam, potato, and a cup of hot mint beverage. Yep! That's it! Actually, from that point forward, a cup of hot mint or marijuana beverage and a slice or two of roasted breadfruit, yam, or potato was all we had for breakfast.

Oh, before I forget, here is a little flash-back humor. That morning my brother must have said something to our father regarding the meal because I overheard him giving my brother a stern reprimand. He told him that there was no way he was going to allow us to bring the Babylonian way of life into his house. He also reminded us that we should leave Pope Paul in Rome. Concerning my brother and I eating Babylonian meals at the orphanage, we were guilty as charged. However, as it relates to the pope, that was something of a mystery to us. In other words, we had no clue who or what our father was talking about. I can assure you that my father was right there when the man escorted us home. Therefore, I am not sure why he was accusing us of bringing the pope home with us. Who knows, probably my brother caused our father to get upset by asking him, "Where's the beef?" Little did he realize that our father had a lot more bones to pick with him. Anyway, regardless of the sudden change of diet, that morning we had no other choice but to enjoy our father's ital breakfast with grace and dignity.

Chapter 3

As you can see, my father did not implement a smooth Babylon-to-Zion transition. One thing that we were all aware of is that our father did not deviate from his Rastafarian doctrine unless he was threatened by the authorities. So, here we go again! After we had been through a rigorous Society 101 Rastafarian cleansing program by the representatives of the Garland Hall Memorial Children's Home, we were once again being reintroduced to our father's strict Rastafarian doctrine.

While living with my father, I did not have a clue of who this Pope Paul person he keeps referencing throughout many of his Rastafarian rituals and chants. However, it was not until my mother-in-law, and I discussed this topic before I finally figured out that all this time my father had been directing his anti-Babylonian chants toward Pope Paul VI who presided over the Catholic Church from 1963 to 1978; as indicated by the Britannica website. Then it all made sense why my father was always asking Jah to burn down Babylon, Rome, synagogue worshipers, and the Pope. According to his philosophy, the Roman Catholic doctrine should be rejected because it was in stark contrast to the Rastafarian doctrine.

Okay, back to the first day's events. After we were through with breakfast, my father prepared marijuana spliffs for all of us, including himself. He told us to smoke them until they were burnt out completely. By the way, smoking marijuana was nothing new because this was the ritual we had before being taken to the orphanage. However, my father included us in all of his marijuana rituals, which will become apparent shortly. After we were through with the marijuana smoking ritual, my father, brother, and I took care of the chickens and the rabbits. We fed the chickens with corn, filled the containers with water, and cut fresh grass and distributed it among the rabbit coops. After we were through with the home chores, our father prepared his tools for the day's farming and carpentry activities. He removed the dirt and other foreign objects from his farming and carpentry tools (machete, pickaxe, hoe, chisels, saws, and more), and then he sharpened them with a file. When he was through, he told us to accompany him to the farm, which was located approximately two miles away from home. Upon arrival, my father lit a fire (most likely to chase the mosquitoes away) before he commenced work. We then relocated the goats to new feeding grounds. Finally, my siblings and I assumed responsibility for the more manual intensive tasks. This was necessary because our father could not do much due to the abuse he suffered at the hands of the police. After a couple of hours of work, we returned home.

At home, my father made a fire and roasted yams that he had harvested from the field. A typical lunch diet was pretty much the same as breakfast. That is, our afternoon meals consisted of roasted breadfruit, yams, or potatoes with a cup of lemonade beverage. After we were through with lunch, my father prepared another marijuana spliff and smoked it by himself. That was a relief for us, especially for me because I had not yet recouped from the early-morning smoking ritual.

Later that afternoon, my brother and I accompanied our father to his workplace. We walked down the winding pathway that led to Mr. Manboard's carpentry workshop. That day I also found out that Mr. Manboard was the owner of the bus that had transported my brother and me home the previous day. Most likely, that explains why

Chapter 3

my brother and I got a free ride. Once again, we were no stranger to this workshop routine because we used to spend most of our days here instead of attending school.

I will now take you through a typical day at the woodwork shop. There were many machines of all sizes and shapes inside the workshop. However, before getting started, my father went through his daily routine. First, he forbade my brother and me to touch or go anywhere near the machines (Safety 101). He then told us to have a seat on a workbench that was located at a safe distance away from the work area. After my brother and I were seated comfortably, our father performed routine maintenance on the machines. After firing up the machines for a test run, he turned off the ones that he would not be using. Finally, he settled down to the work of the day, which included trimming, grooving, and shaping wood to make doors, windows, cabinets, and other household items. However, I could see that my father was struggling to complete the tasks that he had been able to accomplish with no problem before his affliction.

Of all the questions that crossed my mind over the years, the one that amazes me even to this day is this: How was it that my father was able to operate all those machines flawlessly after smoking that much marijuana? I mean, one mistake and he could have ended up losing a couple of fingers or his entire hand. Also, I wonder what it would have been like if Mr. Manboard (his employer) had instituted a drug-free workplace. There would be no need for any urine, blood, or hair samples, because a brief look into my father's eyes would have been more than sufficient.

When my father was through working, he turned off the machines and secured the workshop. After a brief conversation with Mr. Manboard, we went home. Later that evening, my sisters prepared and served each of us a bowl of soup. Like it or not, a bowl of soup was always our dinner, except on rare occasions when my father purchased rice from a local grower. As for the soup, here are the typical ingredients: coconut milk, yams, green bananas, corn, and, yes, a handful or two of marijuana buds was always included. I know you are asking, "Where's the meat?" Well, don't even bother asking. Our diet did not include any meat or salt whatsoever. I can assure you that my father had zero tolerance for meat, salt, and alcohol, but a never-ending appetite for marijuana. After dinner was served, my father took the honor and blessed the meal by giving thanks unto Jah. Once again, we sat down on a small wooden bench and ate our meals. I simply could not believe that before being taken to the orphanage, my brother and I had been eating food without meat or salt. Well, like it or not, we had no other choice but to conform to our ever-changing environments.

If you think that eating ital food was a cause for concern, then just wait until you hear about the next Rastafarian ritual my father introduced to us. Okay, no need to wait, so here are the details. After we were through with dinner, my father took this rather odd-looking pipe (he labeled it chillum and sometimes chalice), filled it with marijuana, lit it, and started puffing away. I do believe that in the USA they refer to this pipe as a bong. According to Merriam-Webster, a chalice is "a special cup for holding wine; especially, the one used in the Christian ceremonial communion." At least my father and the pope had something in common with regard to use of a chalice. Irrespective of their differences, it all made sense why my father

Chapter 3

treated his chalice like a prized trophy and only used it after our final day's meal rather than after each meal. It was like saving the best for last, from his perspective.

The most surprising aspect of this experience was when my father included my brother and me in the smoking ritual. However, smoking marijuana from the chalice did not go over too well for my brother and me. I remember my brother took one puff and immediately started coughing. He quickly handed it off to me like a hot potato, or more like a "hot pot." I wanted to take a pass, but with my father looking on, I had to take a couple of puffs too. Ladies and gentlemen, I almost coughed my lungs out. I was relieved when my father had a "food for thought" moment and decided not to pass it around to my brother and me a second time. My father and my sisters continued to pass the chalice around until the marijuana was completely burnt out.

I was hoping that this would not be an everyday ritual, but I was wrong. In fact, smoking marijuana from the chalice did turn out to be a daily ritual for all of us! My father stated that this was the most sacred way for us to give thanks and praise unto Jah. On second thought, I do believe Jah would have accepted our thanks and praise even if we had done so with a little spliff. My father would put a lot of marijuana seeds in the chalice and, at certain points throughout the smoking ritual, the seeds would burst like popcorn sending marijuana sparks flying everywhere. This madness was like recreating fireworks right in your face. Even to this day, I am still amazed by the explosions those little seeds would cause. I can assure you that marijuana seeds do pack quite a lot of potential energy. We (the children) were terrified because we had no idea when this explosion would occur. As for my father, he found this practice quite amusing. He would go off into one of his "Jah Rastafari" chants after each explosion. In hindsight, we should have interrupted his chant by saying, "Iah man! Your amusing ritual is literally setting us on fire!" Now I know why my clothes had so many tiny holes. It appeared as though I had been attacked by a whole colony of moths. I am beginning to wonder if my father's jumping around after a chalice explosion was really chanting or if he was merely extinguishing the marijuana sparks that fell on him.

I am not sure why my father was forcing us to smoke that much marijuana. Probably this was his way of ridding us of the Babylonian way of life we had adopted while living at the orphanage. Although my brother and I were accustomed to our father's marijuana smoking rituals, this time was different because we had to take part in his everyday rituals.

One thing I know for sure is that my father must have saved the most potent marijuana for his chalice ritual because there were times when it would cause us to experience headaches. Pauline and Paulette told me that they also suffered similar side effects. I can recall on many occasions that my brother and I would let our father know that the herb he was putting into the chalice was too strong. Instead of excluding us from the chalice ritual, he would reply by saying, "Di I dem structa weak!" ("You guys have weak structures!") He stated that our weak structures were directly related to the time we had spent in Babylon (the orphanage) consuming the Babylonian food (salt and meat). Pauline and Paulette also complained to our father in similar regard. Once again, he would simply ignore our complaints.

Chapter 3

There were times when I wanted to say to my father, "Enough of this senseless chalice smoking ritual!" But knowing how devoted my father was to his cause, none of us would dare to challenge his authority or try to convince him otherwise. In fact, his response to our cries was to give us even more marijuana.

The chalice and the spliffs were not the only two ways in which we consumed marijuana. In fact, my father used marijuana as the primary ingredient in most of our meals. He added it to our hot beverages (tea), soups, vegetables, and just about every meal we consumed. Concerning marijuana, I would say that we were the perfect consumers. We ate it, drank it, and smoked lots of it. My father must have thought that marijuana was a substitute for everything, including medicine. If my father were a medical doctor, I could see him writing marijuana prescriptions for all his patients regardless of their ailments.

Although this Rastafarian lifestyle had an adverse effect on all of us, it was evident that it affected Pauline the most. Throughout one of my conversations with her, she told me that, at one point, she had become fed up with the constant marijuana smoking rituals that our father imposed on us. She also said that at one point, she even applied kerosene oil to her hair so that her locks would fall off. As per Pauline, she resorted to this measure because her locks had grown into large clumps and became really uncomfortable. However, none of that had any influence on our father, because I overheard him reprimanding Pauline on several occasions, letting her know that he did not approve of her Babylonian behavior.

As time progressed, this lifestyle became the norm for all of us. That is, we were not allowed to attend school, and my father continued to work for Mr. Manboard as a carpenter and cultivated vegetables and other produce. And yes! He continued to cultivate marijuana, but on a much smaller scale deep into the mountain. This was necessary to keep it hidden from the authorities. After his chickens died, he took it as a sign from Jah and gave up on livestock rearing completely.

My father took great pride in his farm. He was self-sufficient; he cultivated most of the food we ate. Smoking marijuana was not the only ritual my father practiced. My father was fascinated with the use of the Rastafarian dialect, including the use of the letter I. He used it in and out of context. He sometimes used it for no apparent reason whatsoever. This exercise was most noticeable after he was through smoking his chalice. He would go on a shouting frenzy ritual, "chanting down Babylon," as he would claim. He would say things like "Jah! Rastafari, the Most High! I an I liveth! Bun di Pope Paul dem! Bun dung Babylon! Chant dung Babylon!" This behavior would escalate whenever much lightning and thunder were flashing and echoing across the sky. Throughout such times, my father would be outside "chanting down Babylon," shouting his usual phrases, such as "Jah Rastafari. Selassie I! Haile Selassie I, the conquering lion of the tribe of Judah, King of Kings!"

Back then, I had no idea what my father was saying or, most of all, to whom he was speaking. Or better yet, why the heck he was repeating those phrases over and over again as if the person to whom he spoke had not heard him the first time. The way my father was using the letter 'I', one would think that he had it patented. If that were the case then I would be the beneficiary of many royalties from Apple for all their 'i' Products.

Chapter 3

From my point of view, my father's ritual sounded like one big bangarang. However, later on I came to realize that whenever Rastafarians use the words "Selassie I" they are referring to Haile Selassie the first (Haile Selassie I), who was the emperor of Ethiopia. Even to this day, he is considered to have been a noble person within the Jamaican Rastafarian culture.

Here is a dramatized humor regarding my father's chanting ritual. One day my father, my brother, and I were sitting in the open yard chatting away among ourselves. I am not sure where my sisters were, but most likely they were either inside the house or in the little outdoor kitchen. Nonetheless, it was fully overcast with dark clouds and continuous lightning and thunder flashing and echoing across the sky. Throughout such times, my father would go on a chanting ritual. On this day, I do believe he said something that upset Jah because, all of a sudden, a bolt of lightning came within a couple of feet of where we were sitting, struck a sweetwood tree that was located approximately seventy-five feet behind the house, and set it on fire. I had never seen a green tree burn in such a manner before. This was the first time I had ever witnessed such a spectacular phenomenon. For a minute, I thought I was Moses standing at the burning bush. Okay, you know that thought could not have entered my mind because I had no concept of the Bible much less to quote scriptures. Anyway, after witnessing such a strange phenomenon, everyone, including my father, ran into the house for cover. My father remained absolutely quiet for the rest of the day. I mean he did not even attempt a single peep, tweet, or chirp. Every time that I reflect on this episode, I cannot help but laugh because of my father's reaction. And yes, you can go ahead and laugh too.

In addition to his rainy-day chants, my father would make rather large fires with the bamboo he harvested from a bamboo plantation that was located within proximity to the house. I witnessed my father toiling away all day, gathering bamboo for this ritual. Late into the night, my father would set ablaze the bamboo and chant around the giant fire for hours. This process reminds me of a bonfire ceremony except for the chanting. Anyway, my father would elevate his chanting ritual whenever the bamboo would explode and send sparks flying through the night sky like fireworks. And would you believe all that energy was for naught! He never allowed us to roast a single marshmallow on his sacred fire. Well, seeing that we had no concept of marshmallows, I would like to rephrase by saying, our father never allowed us to roast anything on his sacred bonfire, not even my favorite breadfruit. What a waste of energy!

As time went by, my sisters, my brother, and I continued living with our father with not much of a future. We were never allowed to attend school; neither were we being taught any of life's development skills. Moreover, allowing us to attend school was a precondition that had been agreed to by my father throughout the custody proceedings.

Better Late than Never

My siblings and I were fifteen, ten, and eight years old, respectively, when our father finally decided to allow us to attend school. This was the first time that I can recall being allowed to attend school. Okay, why did this happen? Why

Chapter 3

did my father all of a sudden decide to have a change of heart? At the time I did not know the answer. However, based on what is documented in my file, I was able to conclude that this decision was not based on my father's free choice or a sudden change of heart. Instead, the CDA had threatened to remove us from his care after discovering that we were not attending school as mandated. This was really a big surprise for me, and I am quite sure it was the same for my siblings. Sending us to school went directly against the grain of our father's Rastafarian beliefs. My father classified school teaching as a form of Babylonian indoctrination. Therefore, I would conclude that he was only doing this out of fear of losing custody of his children.

Here is how this "going to school" episode began. One sunny morning, or should I say one sunrise (most likely a Monday), my father got up bright and early and told us to get ready for school. Seeing that this was our first school day, he accompanied us to school. We made our first stop at a little building located on a slope overlooking the main road, as indicated in the photograph below. I am not sure if it is the original building and if the name has always been St. John's Infant school; nonetheless, I will refer to it as such from this point forward. I was the first to be dropped off at school.

My brother and sisters were dropped off at other schools further up the road. At the time, I had no idea what schools they were attending. However, many years later, Paulette told me that she and Pauline were attending a JAMAL school. JAMAL is an abbreviation for the Jamaica Movement for the Advancement of Literacy. Today, as noted by the government of Jamaica, the new abbreviated term is JFLL, which is the Jamaican Foundation for Lifelong

The Adventurous Homecoming

Learning. This literacy development program is geared toward the advancement of youths and adults. My sisters were placed in this program because they were fifteen years old and were unable to read or write. To further complicate the matter, my father was unable to produce copies of our birth records, not even the short forms. Therefore, we were placed at schools and in grade levels based on how old we appeared to be at the time. As for my brother, even to this day, nobody knows which school he attended.

Okay, let's find out how my first school day commenced. Upon arrival, the teacher took me to my classroom and told me to have a seat. I am not sure what name I was registered under but, knowing my father, he must have registered me under my Rastafarian name (Iah). Even if he had registered me under my correct name, it would not have made a difference. I was simply there to fill a void, because my father had not provided me with any school supplies. Not even a pencil or a sheet of paper! I remember sitting in the classroom, not having the slightest clue what the teacher was saying or the significance of why I was there in the first place. Besides, I was feeling sleepy from the hangover triggered by the excessive marijuana smoking ritual.

After sitting there for a while, I heard the bell ring. Credit to the orphanage, I was now acutely aware of the significance of this instrument. However, I came to understand that in this setting, the ringing of the bell signified the commencement of the school day, break periods, lunch hour, and the conclusion of the school day. I remember sitting in the classroom throughout the break and lunch periods. Probably because I was the most interesting kid at school, no one wanted to socialize with me. My father did

Chapter 3

St John's Infant School located in the district of Darliston, Westmoreland, Jamaica. Picture of 2009.

not provide me with any lunch or snacks, so after breakfast, I had to wait until dinner was served.

I remember going to school each day with absolutely no school supplies. It was the same for my siblings. My father did everything to hinder our ability to learn. He did not care to have us learn anything! He was only adhering to the mandate stipulated by the CDA. Besides, he did not believe in what was being taught by the schools in the first place. The only book that was in our house was a particular version of the Bible that my father read occasionally. I am not sure what version my father had but, according to my sisters, our father would read a verse or two as part of his daily ritual. Wouldn't it be nice if we (the children) had been able to read a verse or two as well? Once again, attending school each day with absolutely no resources became the routine for us.

The Adventurous Homecoming

I am not sure of the exact duration of our school experience, however Paulette and Pauline informed me that we were allowed to attend school for approximately four to six weeks. Regardless of the duration, I distinctly remember that our schooling came to an abrupt end when our father told us that he was no longer sending us to the Babylonian place. He allowed us to attend school long enough to convince the CDA that he was serious about sending us to school.

Back to the Old Ways of Life

My father yanked us out of school and told us that we were being led away from the truth. Even to this day, I have no idea what truth we were being led away from. Moreover, we had only attended school for approximately four to six weeks, which was not enough time for us to grasp the basic academic fundamentals. My brother and I had not stayed in school long enough to even learn the letters of the alphabet. Even if my father had provided me with all the required textbooks, notebooks, pens, and pencils, it most likely would not have made a difference because I was always sleepy and in a daze from the constant marijuana smoking.

It is quite difficult for me to understand my father's rationale. He failed to keep his side of the agreement even though the CDA had been willing to overlook all of his other Rastafarian doctrines, even the marijuana smoking ritual. My father refused to compromise in this regard even when Mr. and Mrs. Manboard (his trusted employers) pleaded with him to allow us to attend school.

As you might have noticed, I have not mentioned going to church because my father did not believe in church ritual. He rebuked, chastised, and even despised those who

Chapter 3

professed Christianity. In fact, he told us that church and synagogue followers were hypocrites and pagans.

Despite not being allowed to attend school, Paulette would find a way to continue teaching my brother and me the letters of the alphabet. However, she could only do so while our father was away from home. Here is how a typical session would unfold. Pauline would be on the lookout while Paulette would use the little resources that she had to teach us to recite and write the letters of the alphabet. Whenever Pauline would see our father coming, she would signal to Paulette by saying, "Iah man deh come" ("Iah is coming"). With much haste, Paulette would make sure that all the papers and the pencils were tucked away safely in a drawer or a secluded place.

One day my father came home and saw Paulette teaching my brother and me. He was deeply upset with her for entertaining the Babylonian doctrine in his house. Sure enough, that triggered the end to our homeschooling. I am not sure why my father was so upset with us for taking the initiative to learn. Why was it not acceptable for us to be seen with a single sheet of paper and a #2 pencil, while I distinctly remembered seeing my father scribbling much-needed information into his notebook with his gigantic #8 pencil? (I am not sure about the pencil size, but I believe #8 is a good guess.)

All I got out of the short-lived homeschooling was the ability to recite a couple of letters from the alphabet. If only Pauline had not left her lookout post unattended, within a couple of weeks, I would have had all the letters of the alphabet fully memorized and become a fluent reader. Well, that would definitely not be the case because, at the pace I was learning, it would have taken more like a

The Adventurous Homecoming

couple of months for me to recite the letters of the alphabet correctly. By the way, please ignore the fluent reader claim because that would certainly not be the case.

On a more somber note, the consequences of our father's action presented us with a lifetime of academic challenge. It breaks my heart to know that Pauline and Paulette were trying to acquire their elementary education throughout their adolescent years. Even when they had the opportunity to attend school, they were forcefully removed because they were unable to keep up with their peers. As for my brother and me, we suffered severe consequences at the hands of our foster parents for not having the academic requirements children our age should have.[5]

Although I do not have the scientific proof to substantiate my claim, I firmly believe that the constant marijuana smoking along with missing out on our early childhood education severely diminished our ability to learn at the average pace. Throughout my entire academic career and even to this very day, when compared to the average child, I have to spend three to four times the number of hours studying to overcome this limitation. It is quite difficult for me to accept or even begin to understand my father's rationale as it relates to his children. Why a father who was given the opportunity to acquire basic education would deny his children such an opportunity! According to information documented in my file by the CDA, my father would provide the agency with silly, made-up excuses why he would not allow us to attend school. One of which was that we had lice in our hair.

---

[5] I have elaborated on this, and many other unintended consequences, in volumes 2, 3, and 4 of my autobiography.

Chapter 3

Today, my experiences cause me to question one's motive in situations where one indulges in an ideology that compromises the well-being of children! I do believe that, as parents, we need to take a moment and ask ourselves where on our list of priorities the well-being of our children is ranked. In other words, as parents, are our dreams and aspirations more important than the well-being of our children? Although I am a bit upset, I must always remind myself that I should reserve my judgment because I do not have the full understanding of why my father resorted to a lifestyle that was at odds with societal norms.

We were being isolated from the outside world. We were never allowed to go anywhere or to talk to anyone unless we were accompanied by our father. In fact, we only went where he went and spoke to those with whom he spoke. My sisters' daily routine involved going back and forth between the home and the farm. I believe that my father resorted to those measures because he was concerned that the authorities would remove us from his care.

Occasionally, our routine would be interrupted when my brother and I had to participate in a marijuana smoking ritual hosted by our father and a number of his Rastafarian brethren. This activity would take place at our home or at one of our father's brethren's homes. This get-together ritual is similar to the American potluck ritual. Now that I think about it, my father and his brethren should have used the term potluck, because it is more fitting for their occasion. Here is how a typical get-together ritual would unfold. First, my father and his brethren would exchange marijuana or herb (cured/dried marijuana), as per the Rastafarian tradition. It was as if they were having a contest among themselves to uncover who had the most potent herb.

The Adventurous Homecoming

According to my father's brethren, my father had the best herb every time. I remember overhearing my father receiving quite a lot of accolades from his brethren. In fact, they would commend him by saying, "Iah man, dis yah a good herb, man." ("Iah, man, this marijuana is the best!") However, in most cases, it was not the same reaction my father had concerning his brethren. In fact, he was highly upset when he found out that he was exchanging his prize herb for inferior ones. On several occasions, I overheard my father complaining, saying things like, "A wah kina herb dis yah Natty give di I?" ("What kind of herb is this that Natty/brethren give me?") I believe my father's brethren were only showing up at the rituals just to receive his potent herb. I guess they had no interest in cultivating good herb when all they had to do was to show up at an all-you-can-smoke ritual and enjoy the best marijuana.

Although I had no real concept of time back then, I would surmise that we spent an average of three to four hours at night smoking marijuana and chanting down Babylon. I was never fond of attending the rituals that were held at my father's brethren's homes. Walking home at night was always a daunting task for my brother and me. In fact, we had to walk through the woods instead of on the road. I had no idea how I made it home because it felt as though I was always floating instead of walking. However, the floating effect was just an illusion because every so often, my father would beckon to my brother and me by saying, "Iah, man, step up!" Before I conclude this section, I would like to share a little ghost humor with you.

One night while we were on our way home from one of our rituals, my father stopped in the middle of the woods and said, "Iah, man, di I was attacked by a ghost at dis spot di adder night." ("I was attacked by a ghost at this very place the other night.") I am not sure what was going on in my brother's mind, but as for me, it did not make a difference because at the time I had no real concept of ghosts or who or what my father was talking about. In hindsight, I should have said to my father, "Iah, man, you pick a fine time to tell us about your ghost encounter!" Or better yet, "Iah, man, you smoked a little too much of your brethren's crappy herb."

Despite the ghost episode, back then I was quite curious why my father would choose to walk through the woods rather than on the nicely paved roads. I found out later that he did so because he did not want the police to confiscate his prize marijuana. I can assure you that throughout such times, my brother and I were always tired, sleepy, and, most of all, exhausted from all the marijuana smoking rituals. Although we despised our father's rituals, we could not let him know or display any lack of interest.

The Unexpected

Once again, it was another sunny morning when we were at home, going about our daily routine. Pauline and Paulette were in the kitchen preparing breakfast while my father, my brother, and I were sitting down relaxing under a tangerine tree that was within proximity to the kitchen. While we were chitchatting among ourselves, waiting for breakfast to be served, we heard footsteps and voices coming toward us from down the little dirt path. Seeing that our home was located at the very end of the trail, this was a clear indication that the person or persons we heard were on their way to pay us a visit. Lo and behold, it was

The Adventurous Homecoming

like déjà vu all over again when several police officers (two men and a woman) appeared before us.

Immediately, my father said in a loud voice, "Morning, officers." My father raised his voice so that my sisters could get rid of the marijuana that was strung out all over the kitchen. Immediately, the police officers started searching the house, kitchen, and the surrounding areas. However, they did not find any substantial amount of marijuana to warrant an arrest. This time my father did not have any marijuana plantations within proximity to the home, so there was no reason for him to be concerned and, most likely, no reason for the police officers to physically abuse him as they had done on their first visit. I do believe that my father had learned his lesson quite well. This time around, he had his marijuana plantation hidden deep in the bushes so that it was virtually impossible for the police to find it.

However, the police officers removed us (my two sisters, my brother, and me) from our father's care because he had violated the terms of the custody agreement; that is, not allowing us to attend school as stipulated by the CDA. As we were being led away by the police, I could hear my father pleading his case. Despite my father's desperate pleas, the police took us from his care, and I did not see or hear from him until fourteen years later.

Cause for Concern

Although I do not fully understand why my father resorted to such lifestyle, in hindsight, I wish he had taken a more responsible approach to the well-being of his children! I wish he had allowed us to attend school and had not forced us to consume that much marijuana! And most important, I wish he had realized that the upheavals were causing physical and psychological harm to his children!

I believe that the continuous consumption of marijuana contributed to our mental deficiencies. One of which is our inability to process and retain information as normal children. Even after my sisters were no longer in our father's care, they were also removed from school because of their inability to meet the basic academic requirements. It is heartbreaking for me to imagine how devastating that must have been for them. Twice my sisters were denied the opportunity of acquiring the basic education. First, by our father, and second, by the decisions made on their behalf by society. Paulette told me that most of what she and Pauline learned came through being self-taught. They realized and acknowledged the importance of being able to read and write and pushed themselves to pick up books and read. I wish I had been in a position to have done more for my siblings. These are the ripple effects of our fathers' strict ideology. Every time that I reflect on my fathers' actions, it undoubtedly causes me much emotional grief. However, I must reserve my judgment because I do not have a full understanding of why my father resorted to such a lifestyle. Could it have something to do with the injustices of his time? Could it have something to do with how one race of people was considered and treated as inferior to the other? I wish I had the opportunity to discuss with my father the reason why he had embraced such ideology.

After witnessing what had happened to my father, and later realizing that the abusive actions taken by the police officers were directly related to him cultivating marijuana, I promised myself that as long as I live, I would have nothing to do with such an evil plant. However, as it relates to the United States of America, it appears as though the perceived economic incentive is one of the benefits that can no longer be ignored. As of June 2019, 33 states and the District of Columbia had legalized marijuana for medical and or recreational use (Governing).

With that being said, I can't help seeing the irony. That is, after incarcerating thousands of offenders and after spending millions of dollars to eradicate marijuana from countries such as Jamaica, I would never have imagined that the very same practices (cultivation and consumption of marijuana) once perceived to be harmful and pose a direct threat to society would one day be considered legal in the United States of America. And come to think of it, the untimely death of my father was one of the unintended consequences that resulted from the marijuana eradication program. In fact, there were times when the Jamaican skies were buzzing with helicopters hovering around searching for marijuana plantations. Upon enquiry, I was told that this operation was one aspect of the marijuana eradication program coordinated by the United States of America and the Jamaican Drug Enforcement Authorities.

My father embraced the consumption of marijuana as a means by which he paid reverence to the Rastafarian doctrine. He also instilled in his children, the need to adhere to this religious practice. The frequency and quantity of use were left solely to my father's discretion. Therefore, this ritual was practiced without taking into account the unintended consequences as it related to our health and our social developmental needs. For example, we suffered the adverse effects of a broken home, isolation, separation,

Chapter 3

and many other unintended consequences. My father paid a heavy price at the hands of the authorities for cultivating marijuana. He had his children removed from his care. He was jailed, severely beaten, which contributed to his many years of suffering and, eventually, his untimely death.

Based on my experiences, I would like to recommend that the legalization of marijuana *not* be viewed with a gold-rush mentality or as just a measure on a ballot. Instead, a life-changing decision such as this should be made through a thoughtful and well-researched process. If parents were allowed to adopt philosophies that are similar to that of my parents, especially my father, then I could envision many unintended physical, social, and psychological consequences relating to the use and or abuse of marijuana. Although I do not have the scientific or legal rationale to support the decision whether to legalize or not to legalize the use of marijuana, the evidence reveals that the current system that deemed to criminalize the use of marijuana is surely not the correct approach. Too many lives, especially those of curious minors, are being ruined in the process. I would rather have a system that educates, rather than one that is quick to incarcerate; thus contributing to other forms of physical and or psychological abuse. The system should not cause more harm to the very ones it sets out to protect from the effects caused by the abuse of marijuana. My father is a prime example of one who was victimized by the system.

CHAPTER 4

BACK IN THE HANDS OF THE AUTHORITIES

So, here we go again! As we were being escorted off the mountain, I could see the curious residents coming out of their homes to observe the process as it unfolded for a second time. We knew we were being separated from our father, but we had no idea where they were taking us. The minute we arrived at the main road, we were quickly escorted into one of the police vehicles and, once again, driven off into the great unknown.

This time around, the police did not look happy at all. I overheard one of them inquiring of my sisters if they knew where our father's marijuana plantation was. Most likely, they were the very same police officers who had harvested my father's marijuana during their first visit. I just hoped that they were not mad at us because it was not our fault that they were leaving empty-handed. We knew where our father planted his marijuana, but that was not something we would disclose. Not after witnessing what they did to our father on their first visit.

As for the motor vehicle ride, this time I did not experience any of the weird up-and-down motion sickness. The Toyota-made vehicle was doing exactly what it

Chapter 4

was designed to do. That is, "moving forward" and "going places." And this time around, I can truly say, "I love what you do for me, Toyota." Okay, a little too much advert, but I simply could not help myself. Nonetheless, a little humor here and there helps to ease the psychological pain.

Our destination became known when the police vehicle turned off the main road onto a little side street and finally into the driveway of a very familiar building. Once again, my brother and I found ourselves being dropped off at the Garland Hall Memorial Children's Home in Anchovy, St. James. As soon as we arrived at the orphanage, one of the police officers opened the door and beckoned to my brother and me to come out of the vehicle. We did accordingly, and the police officer escorted us into the building.

Auntie came out onto the verandah and said something to the effect of, "Look! It is the two Nyah pickney dem again." I believe that Auntie was not looking forward to our return visit. No sir! Not after doing such an excellent job ridding us of the Rastafarian lifestyle. She was quite surprised when she noticed that we were once again sporting dreadlocks. Poor Auntie. I could just imagine what must have been going through her mind. She probably was thinking, "Lord, why me? Have I not taken these two boys and scrubbed the Rastafarian lifestyle from their minds, bodies, and souls? Have I not introduced them to society and a state of normalcy? Have I not? And now I will have to go through this process all over again?" I am quite sure there must have been a thousand "Have I not" questions going through her mind when she saw my brother and me driven into town for the second time. Well, I do believe Auntie had no other choice but to get used to the idea of having us around. And, as you are quite aware, this was certainly not our first visit and probably might not be our last either. Stay tuned because the revelation will come to pass shortly.

Before I proceed, let's find out what decisions were made on behalf of my sisters. My sisters told me many years later that they were taken to an all-girl orphanage located in Granville, Trelawny. After spending approximately two and a half years at this orphanage, they were then transferred to another orphanage in Kingston. Now that we know what happened to my sisters, it is time to uncover what challenges my brother and I faced throughout our second visit to the orphanage.

The transition process commenced with Auntie's beckoning to one of the women who worked at the orphanage to accompany us to the back. Seeing that this was our second time being taken to the orphanage, we did not experience the dramatic culture shock that we had on our first visit. However, despite not being a stranger to the system, it was still difficult to find ourselves being separated from our father and sisters.

Once again, we were summoned to go and take showers. My brother and I remembered the drill, so we went directly to the bathroom, showered, and dressed in the usual orphanage attire. Dinner had already been served, so we had to wait for supper. Although I am not entirely sure, I believe we were served bread with either cheese or jelly and hot Milo beverages. In fact, bread with cheese or bread with jelly and hot Milo beverage became our consistent diet for a while because we refused to consume any meat.

After supper, we retired to the dorm. Most of the children, including Denham, the McDonalds (twin boys, we

Chapter 4

addressed them as Fat Twin and Meager Twin), Butty, Garnett, Otis, Joy, and Marlene were still at the orphanage. They also remembered our Rastafarian pet names, Red Nyah and Black Nyah. That night, one of the older boys took a pair of scissors and gave my brother a partial haircut. Boy oh boy! He did a really botched job on George's head. After observing what was done to my brother's hair, I decided that it was not a good idea to let them mess with mine. No sir! I would rather take my chances with a real barber.

Anyway, we talked for a while, mostly in the "I an I" dialect, but this time around with less drama. That is, our communication was no longer significantly deficient, at least from my perspective. However, the boys who had been at the orphanage for our first visit were the ones asking most of the questions. Before I continue, I would like for you to pay close attention to the words *significantly deficient* because they will reappear sometime in the distant future.

After the drama was over, we all retired to bed. The next morning my brother and I got up, went outside, and socialized with the other boys who were already up and about. That is, we talked and shared a few laughs while we assisted with the morning chores. Shortly after that, the breakfast bell rang, and the children, including my brother and me, ran into the dining room. My brother and I had not eaten any meat or salt in more than a year, so we only ate the bread and drank the hot Milo beverage. I am not sure for how long we maintained this meatless diet, however, what I do know is that as time progressed, we gradually conformed to the daily meat and salt diet. The transition process was much smoother than our first visit and involved less drama as well.

Back in the Hands of The Authorities

After breakfast, my brother and I were taken to the barber so that we could have our dreadlocks trimmed. As for the barber episode, everything was similar to our first visit except that this time around I did not put up a fight. Concerning my brother, it must have been an easy task for the barber because George had already had a good portion of his hair hacked off by one of the boys at the orphanage.

Seeing that this was our second visit to the orphanage, I will provide you with a summary of the outstanding events instead of the intricate details. While at the orphanage, it was a joy to witness the representatives from the many charitable organizations as they graced us with occasional visits. I remember my brother and I would sit at the front of the building overlooking the main road, observing the vehicles go by. We were thrilled whenever a vehicle or set of vehicles would turn off the main road and onto the little side street that led to the orphanage. Witnessing the vehicles coming up the driveway was always a good indication that we were about to receive a snack or two that day.

It was important to be at the head, or as close as possible to the head, of the queue. Here is why: There were instances when my brother and I would notice a number of the children coming out of the hall or living area with snacks. We would run into the hall as quickly as we could but "Too late!" would be our cry because all the snacks were already gone. It's ok to go ahead and say "Aww," because none of the other children were willing to share their snacks with us. Not only that, but they would repeat the most conservative Jamaican phrase: "Who beg nah get, an who nuh beg nuh want." ("Those who ask will not receive, and those who do not ask do not want any.") Whenever I was fortunate to get a pack or two of cookies, I would let one pack serve me for a whole day. First, I would separate the cookies, then I would lick the filling from both sides (ooh, tasty), then I would put them back in the bag, and from there I would nibble on them ever so slowly.

Okay, enough of the snack drama, let's move on to Christmas. No other day was more important than Christmas day when we received our elegant, all-inclusive meal. Such a treat was made possible by the Lions Club and the Kiwanis charitable organizations. On this day, the Lions Club (we used to address them as Lions Men) or the Kiwanis members would come "roaring" up the driveway with vehicles that were filled with food, snacks, toys, and a lot more goodies. A day like this was certainly not ordinary.

The first order of business was for us to shower, get dressed, and congregate in the open hall. Then the charitable organization members would serve us a healthy meal that included rice and beans, chicken, turkey, roast beef, and ham. After we were through with our main course, we would receive a serving of ice cream, a slice or two of the most delicious cakes, and an assortment of cookies. It appeared as though I was more interested in getting a good meal topped off with a delicious serving of ice cream and a toy (if there was enough for everyone) rather than ascertaining the true meaning of Christmas.

Not only that, but Christmas day was one of the rare times when we would get a break from the dry, hard-to-swallow bulgur. Speaking of bulgur, here is a fact that I would like to share. According to Sunnyland Mills ("America's bulgur company"), "Bulgur is a nutritious, versatile wheat product with a pleasant, nut-like flavor." While living at the orphanage, I was accustomed to eating bulgur five days a week, which technically makes me a bulgur expert; therefore, I am not sure about this "pleasant, nut-like flavor" that Mr. Sunnyland Mills is gloating about.

Okay, enough of Mr. Sunnyland Mills, I will now get back to my delicious, bulgur-free Christmas dinner. After we were through with our main course and our tasty desserts, we joined the queue and prayed that we were close enough to receive a gift from Santa. In addition to the delicious meals and toys, the club members would take several children on field trips. My brother and I were never fortunate enough to have gone on any of the field trips. (this could have had something to do with my previous attempt to run away from the orphanage.) From what we heard, the children who had the opportunity were taken to the Hope Gardens Zoo in Kingston and to other scenic places around the island.

Once again, my brother and I were not allowed to attend to school. Most likely, it had something to do with our illiteracy. Nonetheless, we get to sit into a room and listen as the missionaries taught us about Jesus and the Bible. However, several mentally ill children were being forced into a room against their will, and they were not happy. To put things into perspective, I will provide you with an overview of one of the more troubling incidents. There was this mentally ill child who, instead of joining the rest of the children at the dining table, he would go directly to his comfortable location behind the kitchen. He would sit there all day, begging for scraps. Every so often, the cooks would give him a little food through the window.

However, on this particular day, when this missionary lady came to the orphanage, one of the workers forcefully removed this mentally ill child from his comfortable

Chapter 4

place by the kitchen window and dragged him kicking and screaming into the room. The minute the man left the room, the child would run through the door and go right back to his place behind the kitchen. This process was repeated several times because it was paramount for the child to sit and listen to what this missionary lady was teaching. However, the child was not happy being removed, so he kept running back to his favorite place behind the kitchen.

As for me, I did not really understand much of what was being said. In fact, I was really there hoping to receive a cookie or two. From my perspective, any white person that comes to the orphanage was really there to feed us. Nevertheless, the things that registered in my mind to this very day are the wonderful and loving attributes that I was told concerning Jesus by the orphanage.

Recognizing My Mother for the Very First Time

I am not sure how long my brother and I were at the orphanage throughout our second visit. However, it was time for us to brace ourselves for another dramatic episode. This episode began when we were summoned by Auntie to come to the verandah. We got up and ran to the verandah as quickly as possible. Upon arrival, Auntie introduced us to a little woman who was sitting down on a chair holding a small bag on her lap. She said, "come and meet your mother." Then she said to the woman, "Mam, here are your sons." The little woman was looking at us the very way we were looking at her. That is, with a sense of disbelief.

I do believe that if Auntie had not introduced us to our mother, she would not have known that we were, indeed, her sons. Nonetheless, she got up, hugged us, and kept repeating our names. She said, "George, Desmond, George, Desmond," several times. Then she reached into her bag, took out a small loaf of bread, and gave it to us. The bread was so small it appeared as though my mother were about to commemorate Passover (Biblical reference).

After she gave us the bread, we talked. No! Let me rephrase. We listened to our mother as she talked and talked. I remember she told us that she had made several unsuccessful attempts to locate us. I am not sure if she had or had not, however, I was not too concerned regarding her previous unsuccessful attempts. Instead, I was too happy to know that she had finally found us and was about to take us home. At least that was what I thought she was there to do.

I did not understand much of what my mother was saying because I was simply too excited and was unable to maintain my composure. I was just waiting for her to say, "Let's go home." Although I had spent many days sitting down at the front of the orphanage looking out for my mother, I had been merely going through a routine, because I had no concept of having a mother, nor did I understand the significance of a mother within the family structure. I cannot recall hearing my father, my sisters, or my brother ever mentioning or discussing anything regarding our mother. Therefore, my only dream was that someday my brother and I would be reunited with our father and our sisters, Pauline and Paulette. In fact, the only time I had ever heard anyone making mention of my mother was when the older children at the orphanage pulled a prank on me by telling me that my mother passed by the orphanage every day. And would you believe that I spent

Chapter 4

many days looking out for a mother I had never seen or heard of before? They sure fooled me!

After my brother and I were through talking with our mother, she told us that she would not be taking us home with her that day because she had some legal matters to tend to first. We had no clue what legal matters our mother was referring to, nor did we care. All we wanted to do was to go home with her. Looking back, I should have said to my mother, "Mom, forget the legal matters. We need to go home with you right now!" Well, you know this is only in hindsight, because back then I did not have the intellect to converse in such an eloquent manner. So, with that said, she waved goodbye and walked away. I simply could not understand why my mother was leaving the orphanage without us. My hope of going home with my mother that day was crushed. I was devastated! I am sure my brother felt the same way too. However, as time went by, our mother made several visits, so we became accustomed to her leaving us behind at the orphanage.

Throughout her visits, my mother always brought a little loaf of bread with her. It was as if we had a binding contractual clause that guaranteed us a loaf of bread on every visit. I wonder if my mother did not know that according to the scripture, "Man shall not live by bread alone." We were boys so, technically, that scripture verse did not apply to us. One thing I know for sure is that my brother and I appreciated our mother's visits. We always looked forward to having a couple of slices of the hard dough bread because it was a lot more filling than the soft, sliced bread we were accustomed to eating every day. However, the above visits were just a precursor of what was to come. So continue to remain seated with your seatbelts fastened because the next chapter of our lives is going to be one with much-anticipated drama.

One early morning, while my brother and I were getting ready for yet another day's routine at the orphanage, the dorm monitor presented us with what I would describe as out-of-the-ordinary formal attire. She told us to shower, get dressed, and have a seat on the front verandah. I am not sure if she provided us with the reason, however, based on our previous experience, we knew that getting dressed and sitting on the verandah meant that we were about to leave the orphanage for good. With that in mind, we showered, dressed, ate breakfast, and went and sat down on the verandah, the place I had labeled the staging area.

Shortly after that, I saw a car coming up the driveway. After it came to a stop, a woman stepped out and, with much haste, made her way up the stairs. She greeted us and told us that she was a representative of Children's Services (CDA) and that she was there to take us home to our mother. She then asked if we were happy to be going home to be with our mother. Not knowing what awaited us, we delightfully and enthusiastically said, "Yes!" After a short conversation with Auntie, she signaled to us that it was time to go. We got up and followed her to the car. She opened the door and beckoned to us to go inside and have a seat. After we were seated, we commenced our homeward-bound journey. The suspense was finally over and we were on our way to be with our mother for the very first time. At least from what I can recall.

CHAPTER 5

HOMEWARD BOUND TO BE WITH MY MOTHER

With this new journey, my brother and I were on our way to add yet another chapter to our roller-coaster lives. After a long ride, the CDA officer finally exited the main road and turned into a complex in which a rather large building was located. I saw many people, motor vehicles, and other activities taking place in and around the building. I also witnessed several police vehicles coming in and out of the premises. The CDA officer drove around the busy parking lot until she found a vacant parking space. After parking, she got out of the car, opened the door, and beckoned us to come out. We did accordingly, then walked briskly from the parking lot to the building.

After navigating around for a while, we finally made our way into an open hall that was overcrowded with many people. I remember overhearing the names of individuals being announced, or more like shouted out, several times by an officer. If the person whose name was announced were present, then he or she would get up, walk forward, and face the judge. The judge would go through the motions and render a verdict. This process went on for a good while. I did not have any concept of courtroom

Chapter 5

proceedings, so I just sat there anxiously waiting to be reunited with my mother.

Finally, it was our turn to face the judge. Or, according to legal proceedings, approach the bench. Although I do not recall the full details, I distinctly remember the CDA officer told us to accompany her. As we approached the judge, I looked off to my right and saw my mother standing there facing the judge also. The judge asked my brother and me if we were happy to be going home with our mother. With no hesitation whatsoever, we responded with a resounding "Yes!" Then she directed her attention toward our mother and reminded her in very stern words that we were now her responsibility and that she should see to it that we were cared for and allowed to attend school. The judge finished by letting my mother know that she should return to court on a specific date to finalize the custody hearing. After a very speedy session, the CDA officer summarized the court proceedings with my mother and then bid us one final goodbye just before she exited the building.

As soon as we walked out the door, my mother found out that she had left behind all her important documents, including her follow-up court appointments. Immediately, she turned to my brother and asked him if he remembered the day that she should return to court. My brother told her that he did not. She asked him to go inside the courtroom and retrieve the documents she had left behind. My brother seemed to understand what our mother was talking about because he went inside and, within a couple of minutes, returned with the documents. She then beckoned to us to follow her as she proceeded to the bus stop that was located across the street from the courthouse.

Homeward Bound To Be With Our Mother

We boarded one of the minibuses and made ourselves comfortable while waiting for the unoccupied seats to be filled with passengers. After the minibus was packed beyond the manufacture's maximum capacity (which is the Jamaican "ram dem in" standard), the driver and conductor were finally ready to leave town. With almost twice the number of allowable people on board, and with the conductor wedged tightly against the door, the driver took off in a hurry, honking the horn as if he were responding to an urgent situation. I was overwhelmed with joy, knowing that we were finally on our way home. Not only that, but I was even happier knowing that I was finally leaving the orphanage for good. Okay, we'll soon find out if "leaving the orphanage for good" happened to be the case or if this were just more wishful thinking on my part.

The driver took us on a daredevil ride, swerving in, out, and around potholes and corners, while making frequent, abrupt stops, letting off and picking up passengers along the way. After the long ride, or what appeared to be, I heard my mother shout to the minibus operator, "One stap, driva." ("One stop, driver.") The minibus came to a stop, and we got off in a hurry. We then navigated a dirt path that led to a little house that was situated on the slope of a hill. Upon arrival, we met an Indian-looking woman who was surrounded by several children. My mother turned to the woman and said, "Sis, si mi son dem yah." ("Sister, here are my sons.") Then she turned to my brother and me and said, "Desmond an George, unnu cum ova yasso an meet unnu Auntie Nel an unnu cousin dem." ("Desmond and George, come and meet your aunt and cousins.") My mother introduced them, saying, "Unnu si Paul, Betty, Byron, Viris, an Eva." By the way, "Viris, Betty, and Eva"

Chapter 5

were really Vyroline, Elizabeth, and Everton, respectively. I was overwhelmed with joy because not only was I home with my mother for the very first time (based on my recollection), but I was also meeting my aunt and cousins for the very first time as well.

So where exactly on the island were we? According to information documented in my file, my brother and I were residing with our mother at Lindos Hill, a little district that is located in the parish of Westmoreland.

Life with My Mother

Remember earlier how I sort of revved you up for yet another dramatic episode? Well, please remain seated because we are about to experience severe turbulence! There we were, feeling right at home in our small studio apartment with our mother, aunt, and cousins. After making ourselves comfortable, we embarked on one of those lengthy "getting to know you" sessions with my cousins, while my mother and my aunt prepared dinner. After we were through with dinner, we talked some more. My mother and my aunt did not own a television or a radio, so a family discussion was the next best form of entertainment we had. Shortly after that, I retired to bed because I had more than enough excitement for one day. This was one of the very few times that I remember experiencing such a dramatic transformation in my life and still was able to get a good night's sleep. I must have been really exhausted from the long day's unusual activities.

Let us go through the first couple of days' activities, which were just a precursor for the more interesting ones to come. Early the next morning, I was awakened by the bleating, chirping, crowing, and continuous barking that was radiating from the neighbor's farm animals and birds. By the way, this is a typical morning experience for people living in the rural areas of the island. In fact, if you happen to live in any of the rural areas of Jamaica, then you definitely do not need an alarm clock because the farm animals and birds are your most reliable wake-up method. Anyway, that morning, I tried to move around on the bed but could not because I was wedged between my brother and one of my cousins. I believe there were four of us on this one bed. So there I was tightly snuggled in the middle with no way for me to get out of bed without stumbling over someone. With that being the case, I just lay there with many thoughts buzzing around in my head. Despite the sardine-like effect, I was happy to be home with my mother, aunt, and cousins.

Shortly after that, my mother got up and went into a little outdoor kitchen to prepare breakfast. Although the kitchen was detached from the house, that did not prevent the smell of burnt wood from wafting throughout the house. The reason for the burnt wood odor was because my mother and aunt did not own an electric or gas stove, so they used dried wood as fuel for cooking. Shortly after that my cousins woke up and started going in and out of the kitchen. It appeared as though they were on a heightened state of alert. They knew that with two more mouths to feed, someone would end up getting a smaller portion, and they were not about to take any chances. Luckily for us, there was enough for everyone.

That afternoon we were not offered any lunch. My brother and I found out quite early that it was not economically feasible for us to have three meals per day. With

Chapter 5

not much to do, we spent the rest of the day being introduced to other family members who were within proximity. Later in the evening, we ate dinner, talked for a while, then finally retired to bed.

Throughout the initial stage, a typical weekday's breakfast consisted of a slice of hard dough bread or a piece of roasted breadfruit with a fried or boiled egg and a cup of hot mint beverage (mint tea, as per Jamaicans). A typical weekday's dinner meal consisted of chicken parts (mostly chicken backs), served with any combination of white rice, boiled potato, or yam. On Saturdays we had chicken-foot soup, while on Sundays we had the Jamaican traditional rice and beans and fried chicken for dinner. Before I proceed, I would like to let you know that the above meal plan lasted only for a short while. The second morning was similar to the first, except that after breakfast, my mother and my aunt went out in search of domestic work. This job search involved our parents roaming the district looking for anyone who needed help with domestic chores. As for the children, we occupied our time wandering around the yard and the surrounding properties. In the initial stage, the daily routine was somewhat consistent except for a few minor variations.

As time progressed, the routine changed significantly. When my mother and aunt went in search of domestic work, my brother, my cousins, and I would spend the day roaming the streets, playing marble games, and engaging in other activities with the other children from the neighborhood. Every morning, except Sundays, we would get up only to discover that our parents were not at home. Most of the time, my mother and my aunt would spend all day performing domestic chores in and around the district.

Their education was limited and they had no real professions, which meant that their only source of income came from whatever domestic work they could find.

Some days they were not so lucky finding work. Instead of coming home empty-handed, they would go by the river hoping to "catch" a day's work from the people who did not have any running water at home and had to do their laundry at the river. Back in those days (the 1970s), only the elite were fortunate enough to afford washing machines. Even today, most people, especially in rural or country areas, still do their laundry by hand.

Withing a number of week, our standard of living started to deteriorate. Our financial outlook became quite dismal. My only speculation is that my mother and my aunt must have been experiencing severe financial issues because even, food became a scarce commodity.

School! What school? So much for the court order and the judge's stipulation that school was of paramount importance. As for my mother, survival was more important, because we were never allowed to attend school, not even for a single day. My mother did not even attempt to show up for her follow-up court hearings. Each day we would roam the streets and, when hunger set in, we would hurry over to the closest McDonald's or Burger King for a double whopper, a large bag of fries, and a 16-ounce soda pop. Okay, I hope you have erased the McDonald's and Burger King reference from your memory because that was only wishful thinking.

Here is precisely what happened: To satisfy our hunger, we would go hunting in the nearby bushes for any available fruits or nuts that we could find. Some days we would go to the river to see if the people who were there to do

Chapter 5

their laundry were cooking or had brought any food with them. On rare occasions, we were fortunate to have gotten a little nibble. Well, it was more like we were privy to the tasty leftover scraps. The days were quite long, so we would do just about anything to occupy our time and suppress our hunger. Other than water, there were many days when a cup of hot mint beverage was the only sustenance we had. If we were lucky, on rare occasions, we would receive a piece of roast breadfruit or hard dough bread. Dinner was contingent upon whether our parents had earned enough money to buy a pound or two of chicken back or chicken foot and a pack of noodle (chicken broth with small pieces of noodles). Despite the hunger, we still had a roof over our head. But wait! Let me not get ahead of myself because that privilege was about to be taken away.

Bye, Bye to the Good Days; Welcome to Life on the Run

This next episode is what I would describe as the Great Depression. I am not sure how long the "good days" lasted, but one thing I do know is that they came to an abrupt end when the property owner came by one morning and took the roof off the house while we were sleeping. I remember waking up that morning not to the beautiful sounds coming from the farm animals and birds, but instead to a strange banging noise, a constant "bangarang" that lasted for a good while!

We did not panic because we thought that the property owner was carrying out repairs to the roof. However, to everyone's surprise, the owner was not repairing the roof, he was removing it so that our parents would realize that they needed to vacate his property immediately. At

Homeward Bound To Be With Our Mother

first, my mother and aunt pretended not to get the message. However, we all got the message loud and clear when the property owner started shouting, "Unnu cum outa mi house!" ("All of you need to get out of my house now!") My mother and my aunt told us to get out of the house as quickly as possible. We ran out of the house and down the pathway with only the clothes we were wearing. I am quite sure that my mother and my aunt wanted to retrieve our belongings but were too afraid to do so.

Hmmm, I bet my mother, aunt, and cousins were living at this home for many generations before my brother, and I showed up and placed a severe strain on the family budget. We all know that having two more mouths to feed is certainly not an easy financial undertaking without additional income. Okay, I must admit that I am not exactly sure what caused the property owner to evict us from his property in such a crude manner. However, based on what I observed before and after, I can only surmise the following: I believe that our extreme hardship situation started when my mother was unable to do much due to an open wound that was located in the palm of her hand. I am not sure which of her hands, but it does not matter because, according to an old saying, one hand cannot wash. The actual phrase is, "One hand cannot clap," but you get the point. Anyway, she had not received any medical attention, and she compounded the problem by continuing to do laundry by hand with the open wound. However, she had to cease such activities when she developed a terrible infection and was no longer able to work. This must have placed a financial strain on the family's limited income. With just enough money to sustain our basic survival needs, my parents must have become delinquent on their rent, thus triggering such drastic action by the property owner.

Here is the irony of this episode. Do you realize that all this time I had thought that the little place where we were living was a house? After reviewing my file some thirty years later, I found out that it was certainly not a house but instead was the property owner's kitchen (according to what the CDA documented in my file). Who knows, probably the property owner was tired of eating out and needed to prepare his homemade jerk meals but was unable do so because a bunch of jerks had taken up residence in his kitchen.

Sleeping Outside in the Great Wide Open

After many hours had gone by, it was quite obvious that our parents had not yet come up with an alternative regarding our accommodation. Although we were within proximity of the house we had been evicted from, I believe that our parents were very much concerned about what would happen if they decided to go back to retrieve our belongings. Moreover, other than the four walls, it was not much different from the outdoors.

That night, we all slept outside on a piece of Posturepedic foam. Well, as my niece would have said, "Posturepedic my foot!" The truth is, the piece of foam was something that had been used to protect valuables while been transported. Now that I think of it, I am curious to know where my mother or my aunt found that piece of foam. Okay, why should I be concerned now when, at the time, it was a blessing to have something to shield my body from the hard ground? Anyway, while we were laying on the piece of foam out in the open, we listened to our parents talking about many things.

As I lay there and gazed into the heavens, I could not help but wonder what would happen next. However, my thought process was constantly being interrupted by the nocturnal creatures that were all around us. Probably they were quite curious and wanted to know why we were invading their turf. That night I had a difficult time falling asleep, which had nothing to do with the insects and the nocturnal animals but was because so much was going on in my mind. The wonderful life I had envisioned with my mother had started to crumble right before my eyes. And the thought of being taken back to the orphanage was now at the forefront of my mind.

I do not recall when I fell asleep that night, however, when I opened my eyes, it was daylight. The rest of the family was awake and talking among themselves. I noticed that there was not even a cup of hot mint beverage as I had been accustomed to when times were "good." I guess I was asking for too much because we did not even have so much as a teapot.

I wonder what had happened to all of our belongings? In retrospect, I believe there are only two possible explanations. First, either what I thought was ours did, indeed, belong to the property owner. Or second, the property owner had confiscated our belongings as a ransom for our outstanding debt. Regardless, all we had were the clothes on our backs and the piece of foam that either my aunt or my mother had been able to snatch from the house.

After everyone got up, my mother and aunt rolled up the piece of foam and told us to follow them. Although we had no idea where our parents were going, we followed

Chapter 5

them down the dirt path that led to the road. I overheard my mother and my aunt discussing the need for us to find a place to live. Finding someone who would rent us a place must have been a difficult undertaking because of our financial woes. With that said, they left us behind while they went in search of a house. Or that's what I assumed they would do.

That day they returned with bad news. They told us that they had been unable to find us a home, not even a place where we could sleep for the night. With no luck finding a place, they decided to take us down to the river so that we could bathe ourselves. Our parents left us by the river and told us that they would be back shortly. Probably they went in search of domestic work. I should specify that it was my aunt who was looking for work because my mother's open wound in the palm of her hand prevented her from doing any domestic work, especially any that included doing laundry by hand.

Later that evening, it started getting dark, and everyone was leaving the river. My mother and my aunt returned to the river and signaled to us that it was time to go. Immediately, we got out of the water and followed them. As for me, I was happy to leave the river because I thought our parents had secured a home and were taking us there. However, after walking for a while, it appeared as though we had embarked on a never-ending walkathon that had us going around in one giant circle.

The real question is why our parents had chosen to roam about in the dark. I believe our parents did not have the financial means to rent a place so they resorted to just walking around hoping to find a vacant property where we could sleep for the night. Seeing that our parents did not encounter any good Samaritans along the way, they decided to take matters into their own hands and started combing through abandoned and unfinished properties. We realized what our parents were up to, so we just followed along and simply went with the flow. However, we were quite exhausted from all the running around and the fact that we had not eaten anything all day except for the drink of thirst-quenching water at the river.

Finally, we came to a house that displayed all the characteristics of a vacant property, one of which was that it had no lights emitting from the inside. Okay, let me explain my rationale. Back in those days, most people living in rural areas could not afford electricity so they would use kerosene oil lamps to light their homes. Before retiring to bed, the homeowners would turn the wicks down to restrict the flames, dimming the light. My mother and my aunt were well aware of this practice and used it as a guide to determine if a house was occupied. With that in mind, they scoped out the house and the surrounding areas while we were left standing off at a safe distance. I can only surmise that they exercised this "wait and see" precautionary measure so that we would have a head start in case they ran into a hostile situation and needed to escape rather quickly.

Back under One Roof

That night, we knew all was well when our parents gave us the all-clear sign by saying, "Children, unnu cum." ("Children, please come.") As soon as they beckoned to us, we ran toward the house as quickly as possible. Upon arrival, my aunt lit a bottle torch, cleared an area in one of the rooms, rolled out the piece of foam, and told us to

Chapter 5

go to bed. Even though the house was in poor condition and resembled an old ruin that did not deter us. We were exhausted from the long day's activities, so we huddled up on the little piece of foam and, in matter minutes, we fell asleep.

However, my sleep lasted only for a short while because I was awakened by the constant moaning and groaning that was coming from outside the house. I found out that it was my mother who was moaning and groaning due to excruciating pain caused by the open wound she had on her hand. Her situation was compounded because she had not received any medical care. In fact, we could barely afford a survival meal much less basic medical care. With that said, my mother and my aunt resorted to just about any homemade remedy that was at their disposal.

That night, my aunt went into the kitchen and made a fire. I was overwhelmed with joy when I looked out the window and saw the flame glowing in the dark. I thought my aunt was preparing a hot meal for us. I could not have been any happier knowing that we were about to receive our first meal in almost thirty hours. However, to my dismay, my aunt was not preparing a hot meal. Instead, she was boiling a pot of homemade (bush) remedy to wash my mother's infected hand. Well, now you know I was only experiencing one of those "thought for food" moments. Anyway, Aunt Nel's homemade remedy seemed to have worked because I did not hear another moan or groan from my mother for the rest of the night.

The Mad Dash

Our sleep was cut short when our parents ran into the house and shouted, "Children, children, unnu get up! Smadi a come." ("Children, children, get up! Someone is coming!") We got up, grabbed the piece of foam and the bottle lamp, and kept running until we were as far away from the house as possible. Come to think of it, we had not been there long enough to even sit down as a family and enjoy a hot meal. Okay, here I am worried about food when I should be grateful that we escaped without being harmed.

It was the beginning of a new day, but something kept reminding me that it was going to be just as gloomy and dismal as the previous day. Once again, we wandered around the district with no real sense of purpose. We spent most of the day at the river and in the nearby bushes searching for any available nuts or fruits that we could find. It was mango season and, lucky for us, we found enough ripe mangoes to subdue the hunger.

The daylight hours flew by rather quickly and everyone had left the river except for us. By this time, the land was dark, and the moon was the only light we had. Okay, I should not be doing a remix of Ben E. King's "Stand by Me," but I simply could not help myself. Anyway, our parents did not want to have us sleep out in the open, so they beckoned to us, saying, "Children, unnu come!" ("Children, let's go!") I knew it was time for us, once again, to go in search of a place to sleep. We started out walking around the district, scoping out the houses, looking for a place to sleep. I was wondering why my mother and my aunt did not go back to the abandoned house where we had slept the previous night. Besides, this would have made life a lot easier for all of us. However, we had left so much evidence behind, it would not have taken much for the owner of the house to find out that someone had been trespassing on the property. Therefore, going back to that house would definitely have been a risky undertaking.

Back under One Roof for Yet a Little While Longer

We kept searching until we found another house that had no light emitting from the inside. My mother and my aunt left us a little distance off while they went to scope out the area. After a short while, we were given the all-clear sign, and we took off running toward the house. Just like the previous night, our parents lit the bottle torch then they cleared an area, rolled out the piece of foam, and told us to go to bed. We had learned to forget about dinner because we did not have any food or kitchen utensils to prepare a hot meal. Regardless of not having received a hot meal, this night was special (at least from my perspective) because we had a small loaf of bread. However, my joy was dampened when I found out that the small loaf of bread was to be shared among all of us. It is times like these that we could do with a little miracle like the "five barley loaves and the two fishes" (a Biblical reference).

    Nevertheless, with my aunt's skillful "breaking of the bread" technique, she managed to feed all of us. After dinner, we retired to bed. Oops, the previous statement sounds a bit too elite, so let me rephrase. After our tiny snack, we retired to the little piece of foam on the floor. I am not sure how many of these "hide and go seek" nights we had, but I remember waking up one morning to a bright and sunny day, which caused me to wonder why we were

Homeward Bound To Be With Our Mother

still camping out on the property and why we had not had to run away like bandits. I am not sure if our parents had secured this property through the appropriate channels or if they had decided to stay put and hope for the best. Whatever the reason, I was relieved that we finally had a stable home.

Not only that, but I was also delighted to have received a cup of hot beverage that morning. It did not taste like the usual peppermint, but I was very happy regardless. In Jamaica, whenever we had no idea what hot beverage we are drinking, we simply labeled it "bush tea." Based on my recollection, the little hot beverage was the only nourishment we had that day. Once again, the day went by, and we retired to the little piece of foam on the floor.

I am not sure how many of these hunger days we survived while living at this house. However, one morning, I got up with my stomach growling from the unbearable hunger. After searching the house and the little outdoor kitchen microscopically, I discovered that there was absolutely no food anywhere. Instead of waiting around for my brother and cousins as I normally would have done, I decided to take a solo trip and head off down to the river in search of something to eat. As I was walking along this shortcut (a path less traveled), lo and behold, I looked through the bushes and saw a mango tree laden with ripe mangoes. At that moment, I thought I had seen the promised land; well, close enough.

It did not dawn on me to stop and wonder how, with so many hungry children around, this mango tree could have gone undetected for so long. But, in the words of Amy Grant, "Baby, I'm the lucky one." With maximum force against least resistance, I took off running toward

Chapter 5

the tree. As soon as I arrived, I climbed up the tree faster than little Zacchaeus (Biblical reference). I reached out, grabbed one of the branches that were laden with golden, ripe mangoes, and pulled it toward me ever so slowly. Just as the mangoes were within reach, the branch slipped out of my hand and snapped like a rubber band. Within split seconds, I felt a whole legion of wasps stinging me all over my hands and face. The last thing I remember was trying to swat the wasps away from my face and falling from the tree. I am not sure how long I lay on the ground, however, after realizing what had happened, I got up and ran all the way home. I guess I had forgotten all about the hunger because I did not stop to pick up any of the mangoes that had fallen from the tree.

My face was swollen to the point that I could barely see out of my eyes. I was running a high fever and experiencing a massive headache. I did not know if my headache was due to the wasp stings or the fall. All I had needed was a mango or two for breakfast but, instead, I ended up with a swollen body and several days of excruciating pain.

Forget about going to the doctor. We barely could find the money for one meal, so going to the doctor was simply not an option. However, my mother boiled a pot of bush remedy and used it to bathe me. And yes, there is a bush remedy in Jamaica for all known ailments. Now I understand why that particular mango tree (the forbidden tree) was laden with ripe mangoes and none of the other hungry children, including my brother and cousins, had gotten to it before I had. The moral of the story is, "Whenever something looks too good to be true, then it is simply too good to be true."

Homeward Bound To Be With Our Mother

Anyway, life went on with no real sense of purpose. Every day we roamed the streets, camped out at the river, and, when hunger set in, searched the nearby bushes for fruits and nuts. One day, out of the blue, this routine was interrupted when we received a long-awaited bowl of soup. This was the first time in a *long* while that we had gotten a hot meal. I emphasized the word "long" because a day is like an eternity to a hungry person. Hallelujah! After waiting patiently, my aunt finally got through cooking. She dished out a small bowl of soup and gave it to me. Boy oh boy! It was looking delicious! The hot steam rising from the bowl with a couple of pieces of dasheen (dasheen is derived from the tuberous root plant family) and chicken foot swirling around in the soup was a mouthwatering experience. After a couple of stirs, I put the bowl to my head and took one big gulp. Ladies and gentlemen, the soup tasted awful! It tasted like my aunt had poured a whole gallon of household bleach into the pot!

Before I proceed, here is a little side note concerning this episode. While revising this section of my autobiography, I decided to do a little research to figure out why I would compare the taste of the soup to that of bleach. To my surprise, I found out that the Centers for Disease Control (CDC) stated, "Adding some bleach helps make water safe to use."[6] This could have been common knowledge but it appeared that my aunt was quite familiar with the "adding some bleach" aspect of the instruction but had no clue concerning the ratio. Most likely, she had added bleach to the water because we had no running water at

---

6 http://www.cdc.gov/healthywater/pdf/emergency/09_202278-B_Make_Water_Safe_Flyer_508.pdf

Chapter 5

home and had to fetch our drinking and cooking water directly from the river.

Anyway, I was too hungry to throw it away, so I remembered taking the sugar jar and pouring a substantial amount of sugar into the soup. That did help a little. However, the sugar gave it a very insipid, sweet-and-sour taste. Lesson learned: sugar and soup do not go well together. I should have called it sweet-and-sour wonton soup. Anyway, not knowing where my next meal was coming from, I consumed every bit of it. It was a good thing I did because that was the last cooked meal I remember having while residing at that house.

Back to our living accommodations: Looking back, I would conclude that we spent a much longer time at this house when compared to the others. Therefore, from my perspective, things seemed normal, and I was happy to know that we did not have to be on the run anymore. Or was I still a dreamer?

I am not sure exactly what happened, but what I do know is this: Life at this "Little House on the Prairie" came to an abrupt end. It happened one day when I noticed that my mother and my aunt were busy packing away the few belongings that we had accumulated. It was quite difficult for me to understand why it was necessary for us to leave after spending all that time there. From what I know today, I can come up with at least two possible scenarios. First, it could be that my mother and my aunt were camping out in the house without permission, and the owner had asked us to leave. Or second, it could have been one of those limited timeshares that we had overlooked. Okay, please disregard the last hypothesis. Regardless of what the situation was, I do believe that my mother and my aunt must have remembered the ordeal we had gone through when the property owner took the roof off the house and chased us out like wild animals. I believe that they did not want us to experience another frightening ordeal. So, once again, we took our belongings and headed off into the unknown like restless nomads.

On the Move Once More

My mother and my aunt waited around until it got dark before making their move. This was done so that we could move about undetected. And yes! This time when I use the word dark, I mean it literally, because there was absolutely no moonlight. We started walking through the dark, looking for a place where we could get a night's sleep. We wandered around but could not find any abandoned houses. Instead of roaming all night, my mother and my aunt diverted off the road and into the bushes.

Not understanding what they were up to, I was a bit curious why we were going off into the bushes. If we had experienced difficulties locating abandoned houses by walking along the roadway, then going off into the bushes would most certainly complicate our search. Little did I realize that my mother and my aunt had long given up on looking for abandoned houses and, instead, had started scoping out the different farms looking for a suitable farm hut. A farm hut is a shelter or shed that the farmers build on their farms to protect their harvest and tools from the direct heat and rain. A Jamaican farm hut is also similar to the Native American Indian hut except the Native American Indian huts were used as their primary dwellings.

Chapter 5

Taking Refuge inside Farm Huts

I am not sure how many farms we scoped out and how many huts we visited that night. What I do remember is that our search ended when we went to one particular farm and found a large spacious hut. It was located deep into the farm, because we had to walk through the farm to get to it. Searching for a farm hut was much different from searching for an abandoned house. Instead of standing a couple of hundred feet away and waiting for our parents to give us the all-clear sign, we all went into the hut together. It must have been very late because we were, once again, very tired and exhausted. I did not know about the others but, as for me, I was ready for a good night's sleep. My mother lit a bottle torch and used it to provide us with the necessary light. Then she and my aunt cleared the debris from an area of the hut, rolled out the piece of foam, and told us to go to bed. As soon as she was through, we leaped onto the piece of foam and made ourselves comfortable.

After we were settled in, our parents told us that they would be back shortly. They left us behind in the hut but did not give us any indication where they were going. Although I had no idea where they were going, the rumbling in my stomach convinced me that they had gone to the local restaurant that was only two huts away. Okay, please forget I ever mentioned a restaurant because by now you have realized that I am still a wishful thinker. Anyway, that night, I decided that I was going to stay awake until they returned. After a short while, my mother and my aunt returned with two small breadfruits. They made a fire in the hut and placed the breadfruits on it. Oh boy! It was one of those hallelujah moments for me! I was overwhelmed with joy because after not eating anything substantial (in this case I am using the word substantial very lightly) for the past couple of days, I was delighted to know that I was about to have a nice dinner. The breadfruits were quite small, and just by looking at the number of mouths to feed, I was concerned that someone was about to draw the short stick.

With that in mind, I was determined to stay awake so that I could receive a slice or two of the roasted breadfruit. However, that night, I made one of the biggest blunders of all times. I ended up dozing off and fell into a deep sleep. And behold, I dreamt that seven meager people devoured the two small breadfruits. I am just kidding about the dream. However, what is accurate about this episode was the fact that when I woke up the following morning, I found out that only those who had been awake were the ones invited to the roast-breadfruit feast. I got up quickly and looked around to see if my mother had left any for me but, to my dismay, the scrapings (instead of peeling the roast breadfruit, you scraped it to minimize waste) were the only physical evidence left behind. I did not even get a slice of the breadfruit. I was extremely upset with myself for letting sleep robbed me of the only hot meal that I could have had in a long while.

Please bear with me while I deviate just a bit to give you a little insight regarding this lifesaving breadfruit. Prior to this writing, I had thought that breadfruit was a native plant of Jamaica. However, after a little research, I found articles that credited Captain Bligh for introducing breadfruit to Jamaica. Irrespective of who or what introduced breadfruit to Jamaica, I am very grateful for this lifesaving fruit because it kept us alive throughout the times when we had nothing else to eat. One of my favorite dishes is roast breadfruit with ackee and dried, salted cod. This meal is referred to as ackee and saltfish. By the way, ackee and saltfish is also the Jamaican national dish.

Anyway, the thought of not getting any of the breadfruits was quickly erased from my mind when we heard footsteps and voices coming toward the hut. Immediately after that, I noticed that my mother and my aunt were scrambling to get all our belongings together. They told us to get out of the hut as quickly as possible. We ran into the nearby bushes and continued to navigate our way to the main road. We had left so much evidence inside the hut; I am convinced that it did not take much for the owner to find out that someone had been trespassing on his or her farm. This certainly was the case because, while I was reading through my file some thirty-two years later, I came across a report in which one of the CDA representatives noted that we were homeless and had been sleeping out of farm huts. So it is quite obvious that we could run, but we certainly could not hide.

Not being able to go back to the hut meant that, within a couple of hours, we would have to go searching for another place to sleep. As the old saying goes, "I'll cross that bridge when I come to it." Or, as it was in our case, we would worry about where to sleep when it got dark. With that in mind, we went about our business as if all were well. Just like any other day, we went to the river where we had a nice long drink of water and a bath, or more like played in the water until hunger set in. When the hunger was too much to ignore, we (the boys) went in search of fruit in the nearby bushes. Mango season was ending, so there was not much to find. However, we supplemented our mango diet with cashews, almonds, stinking toes, and just about any other fruits and nuts that were available and within our reach.

I know you might be curious as to what type of fruit stinking toe is. So, before you go off speculating, I will take the honor of explaining. Although stinking toe has a rather odd name and a not-so-pleasant odor (thus the name), please do not let these attributes discourage you from sampling this delicious fruit. However, you may need to have a glass of water available because it is powdery and can cause choking. Also, I found out that stinking toe is not just a Jamaican label, it is commonly used throughout the Caribbean and Central and South America.

Back to our day at the river: That day, my mother and my aunt camped out by the river, inquiring of the women who were there if they needed assistance doing their laundry. However, it seemed as though no one needed help that morning. With that said, they decided to go off into the nearby district in search of work, or at least that was what I thought. While our parents were away, and with nothing else to do, we stayed at the river and continued to play with the other kids from the neighborhood who had come by for a swim or to assist their parents with the laundry.

I am not sure how long my mother and my aunt were away because we were too busy having fun at the river. However, as the sun began to dip over the horizon, I noticed that everyone started leaving for his or her respective home. I was hoping that my mother or my aunt would return to the river with at least a small loaf of bread because I was starving! To my dismay, they both turned up empty-handed. So there we were, looking forward to enduring yet another night without a proper meal. Reminiscing on

Chapter 5

those days caused me to wonder where we (me in particular because I had missed out on the breadfruit feast) found the energy to keep going after not having a substantial meal in days. Nonetheless, it is amazing how much nutritional value a person can garner just by eating fruits and nuts. I can assure you that those fruits and nuts were our hunger suppressors. Well, "Anything is possible if you put your mind to it." However, I would restate the above phrase as follows: If you condition your mind, then your body will succumb. I will not bore you with each abandoned house and farm hut drama we encountered after that. Instead, I will skip ahead and let you know how the hut-and abandoned-house sleeping arrangement came to an end.

Relocating to Higher Grounds

One day after leaving the river (long after sunset), we found ourselves being led away onto the mountain by our parents. Instead of searching for abandoned homes or farm huts, our parents took us on a trail that led deep into the mountain. We had no idea where we were going because it was pitch dark. However, my mother and my aunt seemed to have known exactly where they were going. I do believe they had scoped out the area in the day and had it preprogrammed into their GPS. Oops, it's Jamaica, and it was 1970s, so please forget the GPS reference.

We had no choice but to follow our parents. We were walking by faith and not by sight because we had absolutely no light. I also noticed that neither my mother nor my aunt had any of our belongings with them. That is, they did not have the little piece of lifesaver foam or the pots and pans they had acquired from the different houses and huts where we had camped out. My only logical explanation is that we had left them behind at the last place we had run away from. After walking through the bushes, around rocks, and over fallen trees, we finally stopped at a particular area on the mountain. My mother and aunt then lit a bottle torch and rolled out the piece of foam at the foot of a giant tree and told us to join them. With no hesitation, we all huddled up on the foam and made ourselves comfortable, just as we had the last umpteen times. At that defining moment, it became quite clear that our parents had already been on the mountain and had secured this sleeping area for us.

After we were all settled in, my aunt took a small piece of bread and divided it among us. In hindsight, I should have said, "What is it about the phrase, 'Man shall not live by bread alone' that you guys do not understand!" Okay, I believe I have used this Biblical phrase one too many times, but I just could not help myself. Anyway, for some unknown reason, I always had a suspicious feeling whenever my mother and aunt would show up with only a small piece of bread. I do believe they had eaten most of it before they got home or, should I say, returned to the place where they had left us. There I was, worrying about portion size and not realizing that the worst was yet to come.

Once again, we listened to our parents as they tried to comfort us with wonderful promises of how things are going to get better soon and how the present situation was only temporary. After they were through talking, we all huddled up on the little piece of foam and went to bed. Now the real question is this: Why had our parents chosen to take us onto the mountain rather than to an abandoned house or farm hut? I believe that my mother

Chapter 5

and my aunt chose the mountain as our final resting place because they were tired of roaming about at night looking for abandoned houses or vacant farm huts. Besides, we knew exactly where we were going at the end of the day.

As for this giant odd-looking tree, I overheard the director of the orphanage mentioned something about my brother and me sleeping under a cotton tree. Many years later, my cousin confirmed that we had, indeed, been sleeping at the foot of a cotton tree. She also told me that the people in the district labeled her and her siblings Cotton Coolie. This name came about because of their Indian-like features and the fact that we were living on the mountain and sleeping under a cotton tree[7].

Irrespective of what took place later, the mountain was now our final resting place. The next morning when I woke up, my mother and my aunt were not with us on the mountain. They had gotten up and slipped out under cover of darkness. When I inquired, I was told that they had both gone to the local Jamaican restaurant to purchase extra-large breakfasts for us. Okay, why do I keep saying these things? Please ignore the Jamaican restaurant reference because that surely was not the case. Well, living on the mountain did cause me to have "high" hopes. Besides, the way my stomach was growling, I would have been thrilled to have just one dumpling.

That morning we did not even receive a cup of hot beverage because our parents did not want to make a fire on the mountain. If they had, then that would certainly

---

[7] Here is a well-known fact regarding the characteristics of a cotton tree. This type of tree typically grows very large, to the point that people carved boats from its trunk.

have blown our cover because smoke tends to trigger curiosity. Therefore, any thought of having a hot meal was totally out of the question. After the morning hours had passed, I set my sights on dinner. I was hoping and praying that my mother or my aunt would show up with at least a piece of bread. Notice I did not mention anything about lunch because lunch was never an option. Not only that, but breakfast and dinner were based on many contingencies that seldom worked in our favor.

By this point, the day was long over because darkness was all around us. Our parents had taken the bottle torch with them, which meant that we had no light, not even a stick of match. Regardless of not having any light, we made ourselves comfortable on the piece of foam. While we were there chatting among ourselves, all of a sudden, we heard sounds like someone was coming directly toward us. We were terrified because we had no idea who or what it was. Shortly after that, we heard a loud sound similar to a dried branch being snapped from a tree. That was enough to trigger our adrenalin, and we took off running. Although it was quite dark and we had no idea where we were going, we kept running because we needed to get off the mountain as quickly as possible. However, we did not get too far before we heard the voices of our parents calling, "Children, children, are you there?" We answered yes, but we had no idea where they were. Within a couple of minutes, we saw our parents coming up the path toward us. It must have been a miracle because, after leaping over rocks and other objects, none of us was hurt. I was delighted to see my mother and my aunt. But most importantly, I was hoping that after seeing how terrified we were, they would reconsider and refrain from taking us back onto

Chapter 5

the mountain. However, to my dismay, our parents took us right back to the place of horror.

We could have been attacked by vicious nocturnal animals because we had no way of defending ourselves. Luckily for us, Jamaica is a lion- and hyena-free island. I guess my mother and my aunt believed that the only way for us to overcome our fear was to embrace it. Anyway, seeing that we had to spend the night camping on the mountain, I was hoping that our parents had brought back large servings of takeout meals for everyone. Despite my wishful thinking, the truth is, food or no food, we always found a way to survive. In fact, on the days when we had absolutely nothing to eat (except for a drink of water), it was always "life goes on," and we looked forward to the next day.

Once again, it was yet another night without food, so we just sat around and listened to our parents as they talked about the good times to come. Or more like the good times they wish we had. Our parents were doing their best to cheer us up and take our minds off the hunger. After sitting around listening to our parents, I fell asleep.

I am not able to recall how we spent each day, but I do remember one particular day when the hunger set in, my brother and I sneaked off the mountain in search of food. We ran down the little trail and into a field that was located at the foot of the mountain. The minute we arrived, we saw dozens of cucumbers hanging off their vines. We ran into the field and immediately started picking and eating the cucumbers. We did not care if the owner was there or not. I guess when you are starving, you think not of the danger or the consequences of your actions because your whole desire is to feed the hunger. I would like to emphasize that there is absolutely nothing cooler, tastier, and more refreshing than cucumbers that have been vitalized by the early morning dew at the foot of a mountain. I can certainly attest to the "cool as a cucumber" phrase because those were the coolest and most delicious cucumbers I ever had. I hope it's not too late to compensate the owner for those delicious cucumbers.

That night, my mother and aunt returned with a small loaf of bread. She summoned us by saying, "Children, unnu cum." ("Come children, gather around.") We did accordingly, and they broke the bread and gave each of us a small piece. Once again, this bread was not enough to quell the hunger but, by this time, we had learned to fill the void with water. That night I was not too disappointed because I had a stomach full of delicious cucumbers from earlier that morning. Besides, I knew exactly what was for breakfast the following morning. Let's just say it was going to be more of the same refreshing, organic cucumbers. Our parents had no idea that we were sneaking off the mountain. If they had, then they would have been very upset with us because they had forbidden us from leaving the mountain. The reason for these stringent measures was the fact that our parents did not want anyone to find out that we were living on the mountain, which explained the reason for their travel patterns, leaving before sunrise and returning after sunset.

As the days went by, things started getting a little better with our sleeping arrangements. Now that I mention it, I might as well fill you in on our upgraded accommodations. One day out of the blue, or more like one night out of the dark, I noticed that for the first time since we had been living on the mountain that we had bed linens to cover ourselves. Although the sheets were quite old and

Chapter 5

worn (having excessively low thread counts), I was very happy to have something to cover with at night.

As for the children, we spent most of our days camping on the mountain while our parents were away. The only exception was when our parents would take us to the river so that we could bathe. Other than that, they would leave before sunrise and return when it was dark to go undetected. The actual time we children spent alone on the mountain was quite long, monotonous, and sometimes scary. Well, no need to worry because our mountain days were coming to an end.

Our Cover is Blown

I am not sure how long we spent living on the mountain. However, I do remember it all came to an end one sunny morning. This particular morning it appeared as though the sun's rays were beaming through the forest trees much more brightly and the birds were chirping more harmoniously than they had the previous mornings. The tranquility was soon interrupted by faint chopping sounds that were echoing through the bushes. It sounded like someone was using a machete to chop wood. The sound started getting louder and louder. I remember my mother and my aunt signaled to us to be quiet. They said, "Children, unnu quiet. A smadi a chap fiyah wood." ("Children, be quiet. It is someone chopping firewood.") As I have stated before, in the countryside or rural areas, dried wood was a source of fuel for cooking and roasting food, especially my favorite breadfruit. Back then, I did not know why my mother and my aunt did not go job hunting that day. However, that speculation was put to rest when I found out that the tradition in Jamaica is not to perform any hard labor (which includes doing laundry and cleaning) on Sundays. With that said, one could see why our parents were with us on Sundays instead of out roaming the district.

As we sat there in absolute silence, the unique sound of someone using a machete to chop firewood began to get louder and louder with each passing moment. It was undeniably clear that the person was coming directly toward us. Before I could catch my breath, lo and behold, a man appeared right before us. I was terrified to see this man standing there with his machete in his hand. This image brought back memories of my father being beaten with machetes by the police.

What was even more surprising was when the man spoke to us in a calm but overly concerned manner. He said, "A wah unnu a du up yasso so early inna di mawnin?" ("What are you doing up here so early in the morning?") Immediately, my mother and my aunt replied in a mutual voice, "We are just here resting for the morning." One would think that they had rehearsed exactly how to respond to such a question. The man, my mother, and my aunt conversed briefly, then he bid us goodbye and went on his way as if he were looking for something specific.

The real question is this: Who could have revealed our secret location? Although I do not know the answer, three possible explanations come to my mind. First, I believe the residents of the district became suspicious of our activities and whereabouts and decided to investigate the matter. That is, seeing our parents throughout the day but having no idea where they were disappearing to at nights. Second, they probably noticed that the children were going on and off the mountain unsupervised and decided to send a

Chapter 5

representative to inquire why. Or, third, it could have been the cucumber farmer who decided to follow the trail after observing that someone was feasting on his cucumbers.

Regardless of what actually happened, the news concerning our living on the mountain spread throughout the district like wildfire. Not only that but, based on my recollection, that was the last night we spent on the mountain. I am not sure how the transition from the mountain to a house took place, but what I do know is that getting our cover blown turned out to be a blessing for us, especially the children. In hindsight, this had not only been a survival-undertaking measure adopted by our parents, but it had turned out to be a compromising situation for the children as well.

Finally Having a Roof over Our Heads

I do not recall all of the intricate details surrounding our departure from the mountain. However, I do remember in the latter days my mother, brother, and I relocated to a small house. Although the house was in very poor condition, I was delighted because we no longer had to roam the district at nights looking for abandoned houses, farm huts, or had to spend another night living on the mountain. Now that it comes to mind, I wonder what happened to the little piece of lifesaver foam that we used to sleep on? I believe it had to have been a piece of memory foam because our parents never left it behind, no matter how urgent the situation was.

After thirty-two years, I managed to track down my aunt and my cousins. And yes! We did reminisce on our not so pleasant, but dramatic, life experiences. During one of our many conversations, I could not help but ask my cousin Vyroline (Diana) how she and her sister Betty had survived those days when we had no home and barely anything to eat. As for the boys, things were a little different because we used to go hunting in the bushes for just about anything that we could find to subdue the hunger. I was delighted when she told me that occasionally a family member would provide her and her sister with milk and roasted breadfruit. Well, well, there I was, feeling guilty that we, the boys, had been quite selfish for not sharing with the girls any of the limited fruits and nuts we found in the bushes. Little had I realized that while we were out in the bushes sniffing around like squirrels, the girls were back at the "palace" enjoying their fresh delivery of whole milk and breadfruit. Okay, that's a bit over-dramatized, but I hope you had a good laugh because I am merely poking fun at our not-so-pleasant past.

Life was not all milk and breadfruit for the girls because my cousin also told me that she and her siblings had been removed from their mother's care by the authorities and taken to Garland Hall. If you recall, this is the same orphanage where the authorities had transferred my brother and me after removing us from our father's care. Now that you know what happened to my cousins, please stay tuned because you will soon uncover what is about to happen to my brother and me.

Back to life with my mother, my brother, and our "luxurious" studio apartment. My brother and I were finally enjoying the comforts of our little home. Everything seemed to be going great. Also, my mother had recovered from the terrible infection that had caused her much pain and suffering. However, having a home and the healing of my mother's wound did not alleviate our hunger problems.

Chapter 5

Here is a breakdown of our daily meal plan: Breakfast was an occasional cup of hot beverage (bush tea), lunch was totally out of the question, and dinner was a maybe. Most of the time, we had no food, except on some days we would receive a small piece of hard dough bread. On rare occasions, we would receive a little bowl of chicken-back or chicken-foot soup. Chicken back, as the name implies, is the back and neck portion of the chicken that comes with very limited meat. As for the chicken foot, there is absolutely no meat to be found anywhere on this part of the chicken! Not sure why people keep buying chicken foot. Probably it keeps them grounded.

Now that we were off the mountain, what was our daily routine? While my mother was out and about in search of domestic work, my brother and I would roam the streets and people's property looking for something to eat. If we were not so lucky to find a ripe fruit or two, we would hope and pray that our mother would come home with at least a third of a loaf of bread. It was always a very disappointing experience (of which there were many) for us to see our mother coming home empty-handed. This outcome was a clear indication that it was going to be yet another long and hungry night for us. Once in a while, our mother would take us to a woman's house where we would get a small bowl of rice or soup. I am not sure if this person was a family member or a friend, but all I know is that I was happy to go to her home just to receive a little taste-bud meal.

Some days we would end up going to the river for a swim because we had absolutely no water at home. My brother and I had plenty of time on our hands. As I have stated before, attending school was entirely out of the question because our mother did not have the necessary financial resource. The way I see it, attending school was surely not one of the components we had in our survival toolkit. Therefore, for the entire time that I was living with my mother, neither my brother nor I attended school for a single day.

Change is About to Happen

I do believe that the people in the district had noticed that my brother and I were not attending school and that we also were roaming the neighborhood like nomads searching for food. Who knows, probably they were fed up with us raiding their fruit trees. Whatever the reason was I am not sure, but one thing I do know is that a concerned resident or residents of the Logwood district notified the authorities regarding our well-being. I am not sure how long my brother and I lived with our mother, but it ended one rainy day while my brother and I were alone at home.

On this particular day, the saying, "When it rains, it pours," turned out to be a true statement. Normally my brother and I would have been "out and about," roaming the district. However, this afternoon we were busy at home, making toy vehicles from the clay we had dug up from the backyard. Whenever it rained, my brother and I would dig the soft, moist clay and use it to make our toys. My brother was the chief architect of the toy manufacturing process. He would make monster trucks, tractors, cars, and other vehicles with fully functional parts. We had to make our own toys because we simply could not afford the ones with the "Made in China" label. I can assure you that my brother had a very creative mind and was quite gifted with his hands.

Chapter 5

Even throughout our later years, he made the bats and balls we used for playing our favorite game of cricket.

With that said, on that particular day, we were busy mining the clay from the backyard and using it to make our toys. However, our mining operation was interrupted when, out of nowhere, a policeman magically appeared before us. When I saw the police, I knew right then and there that my brother and I were about to be removed from our mother's care and, most likely, taken right back to the orphanage.

I remember the policeman shouted at us in a rather loud and crude manner. He said, "Bwoy, a weh unnu mumma de?" ("Boy, where is your mother?") My brother told him that our mother was out and that he had no idea when she was coming home. Based on the officer's tone and actions, I concluded that he was quite upset. Who knows, probably he had come by the house several times but had been unable to locate us. Regardless of the number of visits, one thing I do know is that had it not been raining that afternoon, he would have had no other choice but to come back another day. Anyway, it was like déjà vu all over again because the police officer rounded us up like animals and escorted us to the vehicle.

The police had no intention of waiting around for our mother to show up because the minute we were seated in the vehicle, they drove off with us into the unknown. We did not even have a chance to say goodbye to our mother. However, not being able to say goodbye to our mother most likely saved us from experiencing further psychological pain. The only worldly possessions that my brother and I had were the clothes that we were wearing. We were also barefooted because we did not own a single pair of shoes. Although I did not know exactly where they were taking us, for some unknown reason I could sense that my brother and I were being taken right back to the Garland Hall Memorial Children's Home.

Back then, I did not understand why the police were taking my brother and me away from our mother. It was not as if our mother had a big marijuana plantation or professed Rastafarian doctrine! All that speculation was put to rest approximately thirty-two years later when I had an opportunity to review my file in its entirety. I was able to conclude that the responsible people of the district of Logwood had brought our case of neglect to the attention of the authorities. At the time, I was quite upset with the police. However, today I understand fully why the CDA had to remove us from our mother's care.

After a long ride, I looked out the window and noticed that the surroundings were quite familiar. That was when it dawned on me that my brother and I were being taken right back to Garland Hall. Sure enough, the vehicle turned off the main road and onto the unpaved road that led to the orphanage. When my brother and I were placed in our mother's care, I had hoped and prayed that I would never find myself being taken back to the orphanage again, but little had I realized that it was only wishful thinking.

From that point forward, I never saw or heard from my mother until some seven years later. Please see volume 3 for the details of this reunification. In closing, I can truly say that living with my mother had earned me enough credits to receive a distinguished Boy Scout First Class ranking.

CHAPTER 6

RETURN TO SENDER

As soon as the police vehicle arrived at the orphanage, the police opened the door and beckoned to my brother and me to come on out. We were no strangers to this process, so we got out of the vehicle and walked up the steps to the verandah. As for the director, Auntie, I do believe that the minute she saw us coming, her silent prayer must have been something like, "Lord, what must I do to keep these two Nyah boys away from the orphanage? What is so special about the orphanage why they keep coming back? Why are their parents not keeping them? What . . . ? What . . . ? And why . . . ?" I am almost certain that if Auntie had kept a record of return visits, my brother and I would have certainly been the recipients of such an award. Too bad for Auntie, because we were like boomerangs; we just kept coming back.

I hope Auntie was at least happy to know that we were only covered in mud, because it could have been much worse. We could have returned as Rastafarians sporting kinky, nappy dreads and speaking in the "I an I" dialect. Therefore, Auntie did not need to transform our minds, only our bodies. Our behavior was contingent upon the lifestyle we had been accustomed to before being taken to

Chapter 6

the orphanage. Seeing that our mother was no longer a Rastafarian, we were allowed to speak and maintain a diet that conformed to society's norms. Well, in this context, the word "norm" or "normal" is in reference to our current lifestyle not being bound to the Rastafarian doctrine. However, my brother and I were still outside the norm concerning literacy. For example, we had no real understanding of the numbering system, the letters of the alphabet, or time as it related to days, weeks, months, or years.

Here is a little side note: Although my mother did not practice or uphold Rastafarian practices throughout the time that I spent with her, my sisters and one of my cousins informed me many years later that my mother was the one who had introduced the family to the Rastafarian doctrine.

Seeing that this was our third time being taken to the orphanage, we had the process entirely memorized. We took a shower, put on clean clothes, and made ourselves comfortable while we waited for the next meal to be served. Here is a well-known fact that is worth repeating: Whether it was breakfast, lunch, or supper, if a child arrived at the orphanage just after a meal was served, then, too bad, because he or she would have no other choice but to wait for the next scheduled meal. There was no such thing as snack time unless you were fortunate enough to be around when one of the charitable organizations showed up with snacks. So, after my brother and I were through with the initial onboarding process, we socialized with the other boys (many of whom we knew quite well) while we waited for supper. We did not have to wait long because shortly after our arrival, the bell rang, indicating that it was "supper time!"

The minute we heard the bell, all of the children, including my brother and me, rushed into the dining room and gobbled down our meals. Compared to our previous two visits, this time was much different because we did not have to go through another painful physical and psychological transition concerning our diet. In fact, this time around, we ate everything that was on our plates. If the plates had been edible, then we would have eaten them too.

After supper, we spent some time chatting and kidding around with the other boys. Usually I would experience difficulty sleeping the first night or two at the start of a significant life's transformation, however, despite missing my mother, that night I remember sleeping as if I were right at home. Seeing that we had not gone to school a single day while living with our mother, and only for approximately four to six weeks while living with our father, my brother and I were twelve and ten years old, respectively, and still were unable to read or write. We were clueless as to what time of the day or, for that matter, what day of the week or month of the year it was. This meant that we had no clue what activities would take place on a given day. All we did was follow along.

Our first day's activities were quite similar to what we were accustomed to. That is, we got up and wandered around here and there while waiting for the bell to ring. After a couple of minutes, the bell rang, and my brother and I ran into the dining room and joined the other children for breakfast. In the afternoon we had dinner and, finally, later that evening we had supper. For all our meals, my brother and I ate everything that was on our plates. Too bad for the other boys who had gotten used to enjoying our

Chapter 6

meals during our first and second visits. After supper, we showered and retired to bed. And that was pretty much the routine from that point forward.

Academic Pursuits

Our routine was interrupted one day when the dorm monitor told my brother and me that, the following morning, we would be attending school. I was so excited I had a difficult time falling asleep that night. I can assure you that I was anxiously awaiting my first day of school. The following morning, I got out of bed the minute I saw the sun's rays piercing through the window curtains. Shortly after that, the other boys, including my brother and me, went outside and showered at supersonic speed with the aid of a standpipe. A standpipe is similar to the ones at the beach that people use to wash sand and salt water off their bodies.

After we were through showering, the dorm monitor gave my brother and me school uniforms, which consisted of a pair of khaki pants and a khaki shirt. Forget about sneakers (or crepe, according to Jamaicans). I distinctly remember being given a pair of shoes to wear to church, but none for school. There was just not enough to go around for both occasions. One evident fact was that, whether living with our mother or at the orphanage, if we were not given a pair of sneakers or shoes, then we would have no other choice but to go along our merry way barefooted. However, given the opportunity to attend school was a lot more important than not having a pair of sneakers to wear.

After we were through with breakfast, the dorm monitor gave each of us a half of a notebook (a notebook cut into two halves) and a third of a pencil (a pencil cut into three pieces). She instructed my brother and me to follow the other children to school. As for the pencil, I wish they had given me the piece that had the rubber. Oops! I meant to say eraser. Just to let you know, in Jamaica, we refer to eraser as rubber. I could only surmise that by not giving me any eraser, the orphanage was expecting me to be error free at school. Yeah, right!

After receiving our school supplies, we accompanied the other children and walked along the railroad track (the thing I had once thought was a giant ladder) for approximately one mile to school. Upon arrival, one of the senior boys from the orphanage dropped me off at the elementary school. Seeing that my brother was older, he was dropped off at the Anchovy Primary School and assigned to the first grade. Technically, based on our ages, my brother and I should have been assigned to the fourth and sixth grades, respectively. Therefore, as you can see, we were a tad bit behind our peers. Okay, let's replace the words "tad bit" with "light years."

Many children were playing and having fun in the schoolyard. Seeing that I was the new kid on the block, I just stood there and watched with much anticipation, waiting for the bell to ring. Finally I heard the bell, and the children ran to the front of the building and formed a queue. I did accordingly and imitated the actions taken by the other children. Shortly after that, one of the teachers escorted us into the building. As soon as we were inside, the teacher started the day's activities by taking the attendance. She yelled out the names of each child as if the child were still on the playground. If the child were present, he or she would answer with a resounding, "Present,

Chapter 6

Miss" or "Present, Mam."[8] Seeing that my name was not on the list, the teacher came over to where I was standing and asked, "What is your name?" I told her, and she recorded it in the book and escorted me to my designated classroom. Thank God, she did not ask me to spell my name because I would not have had a clue.

As the school year progressed, I discovered that most of the children were quite friendly. However, a small number of them were a bit hostile and did not care to associate with me. I remembered they would say things like, "Guh weh fram, yasso panzy home bwoy." ("Go away from here, orphanage boy.") They would sometimes go beyond the usual teasing to physical bullying. I was not the only orphan child to have found myself in such a predicament. In fact, many of the children from the orphanage were also bullied and shunned. We were being bullied for no apparent reason other than we were living at an orphanage.

It is obvious that it does not matter where you are in life, there is always a set of bullies jockeying for dominance. Have you heard the saying, "Unity is a source of strength?" For us to fend off these bullies we (the children from the orphanage) had to bond together.

At first, I did not have a clue why the children from the neighborhood labeled the children from the orphanage as ponzi/panzy home pickney (children). I hope Auntie was not operating a Ponzi scheme out of the orphanage, because that would have been totally against the law. Anyway, I decided to probe a little to see what I could find.

---

8 Yep, as children, we were taught to say sir, mam, Mr., Miss, or Mrs. as gestures of respect, especially when addressing adults. Throughout my youthful days, it was (hopefully, still is) a Jamaican tradition to express good manners by addressing elders and people in authority with the appropriate titles.

The only logical explanation was that there were several large poinsettia trees located at the entrance of the property. And, knowing how we Jamaicans tend to find a Patois label for everything, then it would not be difficult to see how the name poinsettia could be easily substituted with any of the those labels.

Despite the occasional bullying and teasing, and the fact that I was not learning much of anything, I always looked forward to the next school day. In fact, the only things that I remember learning throughout the entire time that I was at the elementary school were several nursery rhymes. I learned about "Jack and Jill," "Humpty Dumpty," "London Bridge," and "Ring around the Rosy." Even to this day, I am still trying to uncover why it was necessary for us to recite these nursery rhymes. Or better yet, what their significance was with regard to learning.

As it pertains to Jack and Jill, I would conclude that Jack and Jill were two clumsy children who were unable to navigate steep slopes while carrying pails of water. The person who wrote this nursery rhyme should have visited the little farming district of Sawyers, where I once lived. He or she would have been amazed to see the farmers, especially the women, carrying large buckets of water on their heads while navigating up and down steep slopes to their farms, most remarkably, without the aid of their hands. Not only that, but their hands would be occupied with other farming tools and cooking utensils. As for Humpty Dumpty, I summed up this nursery rhyme with two words, clumsy and reckless! The "London Bridge falling down" nursery rhyme is a good indication that the British should pay closer attention to their crumbling infrastructure. Finally, "Ring around the Rosy" is a reference to the London

Chapter 6

plague, which has nothing to do with Jamaica. Despite my added humor, the one interesting takeaway is that all of the British nursery rhymes (at least the ones I was taught) seemed to signify doom and gloom, which is undoubtedly not uplifting from the perspective of an orphan child.

As for my brother, I am not sure what he was learning in the first grade at Anchovy Primary. I hope it was not any of the mysterious nursery rhymes that I was being taught. Our learning was further complicated because, by the end of the first week, we had already used up the piece of pencil and scribbled all over the half of a notebook. With that said, we spent the rest of the school period with no notebooks or pencils.

My school days at the kindergarten level were short-lived because within a couple weeks, I was transferred to the Anchovy Primary School. What is primary school? In Jamaica, a primary school is similar to elementary and the first year of middle school in the United States. These institutions accommodate children between the ages of six and twelve. Seeing that I was unable to present a copy of my birth certificate (not even the short form), I am not sure what criteria were used to determine that I was too old for kindergarten. Well, it was evident that my outward appearance was quite sufficient. Who knows, probably being able to recite several nursery rhymes was all I needed to be qualified for a transfer from kindergarten to primary. Regardless of the deciding factor, I was now a registered student at the Anchovy Primary School.

My days at the primary school were much different from those I had spent at kindergarten. Priority for learning was paramount. I witnessed children being flogged for not being able to do their homework or in-class assignments correctly. The children who were being punished were screaming and yelling at the tops of their voices. By the way, with regard to the children's screaming, most of the time it was pure theatrics. Regardless, at the time, the screams drove maximum fear into me. I was no longer excited about school. I was very fearful of the teacher and could not wait for class to be dismissed.

I was even more nervous on the days the teacher would give in-class assignments, particularly math problems. She would walk around the classroom and peek over our shoulders to see if we had solved the problems correctly. Seeing that I was illiterate, and my problem was compounded because I did not have a notebook or pencil, I was always guaranteed a beating whenever the teacher asked me to submit my homework. Here is how an unfortunate situation such as this one would unfold: With the teacher fast approaching, I would begin shuffling around, asking the child closest to me for a clean page from his or her notebook and a piece of pencil. I would say to the student closest to me, "Hey, gimi one a yuh book leaf an len mi piece a pencil?" ("Hi there, may I have a sheet of paper from your notebook and may I borrow a pencil?") However, most of the time, the student sitting beside me would reply, "Panzy home bwoy, guh mek yuh mumma buy yuh book and pencil." ("Orphan boy, go and let your mother buy you your book and pencil.") With that said, there was no escaping for me because I would get a double dose of beating. First for not having a notebook and pencil, and second for not completing the assignment.

Let's not be too overly concerned, the main issue was that even if that child sitting next to me had given me his or her entire collection of notebooks and pencils, it would

Chapter 6

Mount Carey Baptist Church. Picture date: 2009.

not have made a difference because I had no clue regarding what was being taught. It is quite clear that the odds were stacked quite high against the children who were living at the orphanage. Come to think of it, my brother had not given me any indication that primary school life was that terrifying. Or probably he had thought that kindergarten was the same. I believe the punishment was instituted as a way to drive maximum fear into the children so that they would complete their assignments and do so correctly. In fact, nobody wanted to be punished and be embarrassed before his or her peers.

After a while, I do not recall being punished by the teacher, which could only be attributed to two reasons. First, either a miracle had taken place and, all of a sudden, I was able to read, write, and solve all of the unknown math problems correctly. Or second, the teacher had long given up on me because she found out that I was from the orphanage where school supplies such as books and pencils were scarce commodities. In this case, I would definitely choose the latter because, academically speaking, I did not know "diddly squat." Or, as they say in Jamaica, I was a "dunce bat." Well, the above statement about being a "dunce bat" is not 100-percent accurate because, despite not being able to read or write, I was able to recite a number of British nursery rhymes. As for school life, that was how it went, and that was the normal routine for the rest of my days at the Anchovy Primary School.

Now that we were attending school, our routine was modified. After breakfast, we would get dressed and go to school. At noon, we would go back to the orphanage, eat lunch (more like dinner), and then go back to school for the afternoon classes (depending on the shift we were assigned and or grade level). After we were dismissed from school, we would go back to the orphanage and complete the assigned chores or just wait around until supper was served. Seeing that neither my brother nor I had any notebooks, textbooks, pens, or pencils, we would join the other children and just wander around the compound until it was time to go to bed. Moreover, even if we had notebooks, textbooks, pens, or pencils, there was no one around to assist us with our schoolwork. We were pretty much on our own from an academic point of view.

As for entertainment, we were allowed to watch television for approximately one hour in the evenings and an hour or two on the weekends. If my memory is as good as it used to be, I certainly remember children's programs, such as Miss Lou (Louise Bennett), "Ring Ding," "Sesame Street," and "The Six Million Dollar Man." I am not sure

Chapter 6

why his price tag had to be that high. Not only that, but think what the orphanage could have done with just a fraction of that money. Anyway, I can still remember Miss Lou's famous folk songs, such as, "Carry mi ackee, go a Linstead Market," and her famous applause line, "Clap dem, clap dem." The famous "Sesame Street" theme song, "Sunny day, sweeping the clouds away," is still buzzing around in my head to this very day.

On Saturdays after breakfast, we were assigned chores that would range from light cleaning on the inside to removing the excess mowed (more like machete chopped) grass from the lawn. Later in the afternoon, we were served a healthy bowl of chicken or beef soup. Sundays were very special because we were allowed to attend the St. James Mount Carey Baptist Church. This was no ordinary church. It was a very big, *más grande*, building that would accommodate a large congregation. The church was located approximately two miles away from the orphanage. It was also quite visible to the public because it was built on a little plateau overlooking the village.

I enjoyed going to church on Sundays. Moreover, it was not like going to school, where the fear of being beaten was always at the forefront of my mind. There were no in-class or take-home assignments except a Bible verse or two to memorize, which I never did because we did not have a Bible, not even a copy of the New Testament. Nevertheless, the most important reason for attending church (at least from my perspective) was the fact that I was quite intrigued by the melodious sound that used to resonate from the gigantic pipe organ. This magnificent instrument and the choir together were superb. Auntie was also a member of the church and the church choir.

After church, we would run back to the orphanage to enjoy our five-star meal. In addition to attending church, Sunday was the only day of the week that we would receive delicious rice and beans and baked chicken, not the hard-to-swallow bulgur wheat. After dinner, we sort of wandered around until supper was served. After supper, we retired to the dorm, and that pretty much concluded the weekly routine.

Throughout our third visit to the orphanage, it appeared as though the facility were experiencing a bit of financial struggle because the meals were much smaller. Just to reiterate, there were no in-between meals or snacks, except when the Lion's Club or Kiwanis representatives would come by the orphanage with snacks.

To satisfy our hunger, we would sneak off the premises and run to Mr. Chen/Chin/Chang's garbage dump for a tasty snack. I am not sure which is the correct spelling, but I will stick with Chen for future reference. As a matter of fact, in Jamaica, most children, and many adults, tend to characterize all Chinese people as Mr. or Ms. Chen, irrespective of their actual names. You might be asking, "Why would the children have a need to go searching through Mr. Chen's garbage dump?" Here are three compelling reasons: First, there was a limited amount of food at the orphanage. Second, Mr. Chen operated a bakery that was located less than two miles away from the orphanage. And third, the bakery employees would dump all the expired products in an open lot that was adjacent to the bakery.

With that said, a number of the children, including my brother and me, would search through the giant pile of baked products for just about anything that was deemed edible. We found bread, buns, cakes, and other

Chapter 6

assorted baked products that were perfectly good to eat. Well, I should not have used the words "perfectly good," but instead should have said that we found baked products that were on the verge of going green but were still edible; at least that was from our perspective. The one good analogy to take into consideration is that these products were environmentally friendly because they were going green. Although they were considered expired according to Mr. Chen's shelf-life standard, we enjoyed eating them because they suppressed our hunger. Not only that, but we were never alone in the bakery dump. There were goats, pigs, dogs, birds, chickens, ducks, and just about any other living creature that had the desire to join in on the all-you-can-eat Chinese buffet.

In addition to Mr. Chen's baked products, we would also go hunting for bottles on the street. We would exchange the bottles for candy at one of the local grocery shops. Every time that I think about this episode, I remember the shopkeeper, Mr. Tingling/Tinglin. (I am not sure about the spelling, but that should be close enough to get the point across.) He would chase us out of his shop whenever we attempted to exchange dirty bottles for candy and or cookies. He would shout at us, "Unnu cum outta mi shop wid di dutty backkle!" ("You guys need to get out of my shop with the dirty bottles!")

The Final Departure

I am not sure how long our third visit to the orphanage lasted, however, based on several positive developments, I sensed that life at the orphanage was about to change for my brother and me. It started out with several visits from one of the CDA representatives. Although she discussed the need to transfer us from the orphanage to wonderful, loving, caring foster parents, we were never given any indication when such a transition would take place. Therefore, I would wake up each day, hoping that this would be the day when it all happened. I am quite sure it was the same outlook my brother had.

After a long wait, it all came to pass one morning when my brother and I were told to take a shower, get dressed, and go and have a seat on the little wooden bench located on the verandah. Once again, we were getting ready to embark on a new journey. I hope you have not forgotten my lengthy discussion as to the probability of what could happen when a child was summoned to the front verandah, the place I had coined as the staging area. Not to mention the incident that happened with the little girl we addressed as Cool Cat, how she had spent all day sitting on the wooden bench but never been picked up by anyone. Once again, it was our turn, and all we could hope for was that we did not reap the same fate as the children who never got picked up.

Being told to get dressed and sit on a little wooden bench located on the verandah did not come as a big surprise to my brother and me because we had been there many times before. It was every child's dream to get dressed and sit on the verandah. However, it could also turn out to be a child's worst nightmare. Whenever I witnessed a child being taken away from the orphanage, I used to hope and pray that my time would come soon. Not to mention how difficult it was for siblings, such as my brother and me, to be adopted. The probability of a child without siblings being adopted was far more likely to occur than a child

Chapter 6

with siblings. Therefore, it was a wonderful experience for my brother and me to have learned that this particular day was our turn. With that said, we ran to the bathroom, showered, dressed, and sat on the little wooden bench that was located on the verandah.

Before I could get comfortable, Auntie happened to look at my feet and sort of knitted her brow. I did not know what the problem was, but I do believe it had something to do with my footwear. Shortly thereafter, she instructed the dorm monitor to exchange the pair of sneakers that I was wearing for one that was the correct size. With all certainty, I do believe that a member of the Bigfoot family had donated the pair of sneakers I had been wearing. Anyway, the dorm monitor took me to the dormitory, took the pair of sneakers from my feet, and started looking around in the closet for another pair. I was happy to know that I was about to receive a pair of sneakers or dress shoes that fit. However, after searching for a while, she was unable to find another pair of sneakers or shoes that fit. I could see the frustration on her face. Finally, she reached over to the other side of the closet (where the female shoes were), took out a pair of white female shoes, and told me to put them on. I wanted to let her know that the shoes she had given me were, indeed, female shoes, but the frustration on her face was a clear indication that I should just put them on and reserve all opinions to myself.

I was very disappointed because I did not know why she thought that it was ok for me to leave the orphanage wearing a pair of female shoes rather than a pair of sneakers that was not the correct size. Moreover, it was apparent that the shoes she had given me did not come anywhere close to the male-shoe category. I mean, those shoes were

100-percent, with no ambiguity, belong to the female category of footwear. After putting on the pair of shoes and making the first couple of steps, I felt as if I were about to tip over. For sure, this was not a good feeling for my Achilles tendons. Despite the awkwardness, I managed to wobble my way from the dorm back to the verandah. I was not happy knowing that I was about to leave the orphanage wearing a pair of female shoes! Nonetheless, I learned to get over my emotions because the last thing I wanted to hear was that I would not be allowed to leave the orphanage just because I did not have the proper footwear.

After sitting on the verandah for a couple of hours (in hindsight, of course), I saw a car coming up the driveway. After it came to a stop, a woman stepped out and walked up the steps and onto the verandah. After a short discussion with the director of the orphanage, she told my brother and me to accompany her. The woman placed us in the car and drove off as if she were in a hurry. I am not sure what was going through Auntie's mind when she stood there and watched as my brother and I were being driven away from the orphanage for the third time. She must have been hoping and praying that this was our final goodbye. Only time would tell if she had gotten her wish. Before we commence the next phase of my life's journey, I would like to make one final but important announcement: Ladies and gentlemen, I am your captain speaking, please remain seated with your seatbelts fastened because we are about to encounter much turbulence throughout the next phase of life's journey.

Thank you very much for choosing to read volume 1 of my autobiography. I hope you have found the first one third of my Jamaican rollercoaster-like life experiences

Chapter 6

interesting but, at the same time, informative. If you wish to explore the next compelling two thirds of my Jamaican life experiences, please proceed to volume 2 and 3 of my autobiography.

JAMAICA - THE JOURNEY

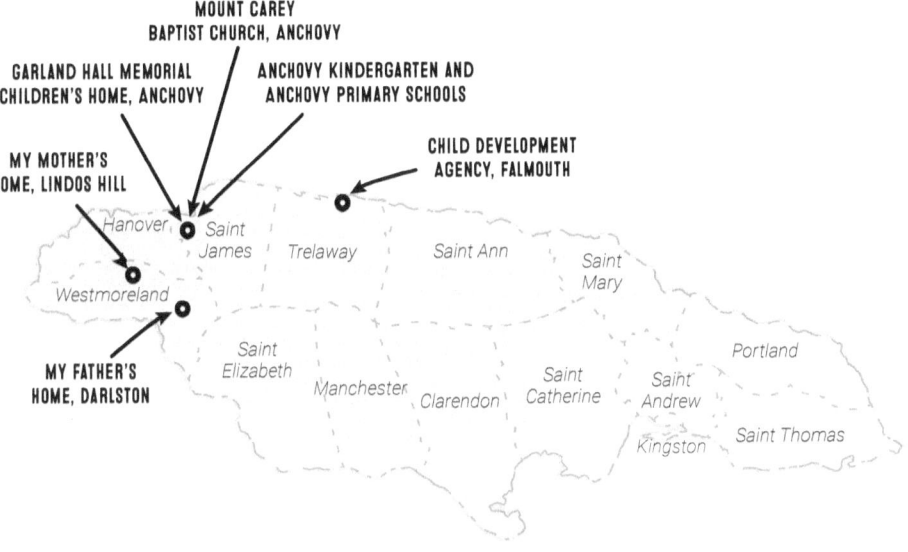

REFERENCES

Reynolds, Ras Dennis *Jabari*. *Jabari Authentic Jamaican Dictionary of the Jamic Language Featuring, Jamaican Patwa and Rasta Iyaric, Pronunciations and Definitions.* Around the Way Books, 2006.

"Rastafarianism." *ReligionFacts*, 16 Feb. 2017, http://www.religionfacts.com/rastafarianism. Accessed 28 August 2019

"State Marijuana Laws in 2019 Map." *Governing*, https://www.governing.com/gov-data/safety-justice/state-marijuana-laws-map-medical-recreational.html. Accessed 21 August 2019

"Hall, Elizabeth (Garland)." *Dacb.org*, https://dacb.org/stories/democratic-republic-of-congo/hall-elizabeth/. Accessed 28 August 2019

www.ingramcontent.com/pod-product-compliance
Lightning Source LLC
Chambersburg PA
CBHW021109080526
44587CB00010B/452